5-Minute Travel Spanish

Berlitz Publishing

New York   Munich

5-MINUTE TRAVEL Spanish

Contacting the Editors
Every effort has been made to provide accurate information in this publication, but changes are inevitable. The publisher cannot be responsible for any resulting loss, inconvenience or injury. We would appreciate it if readers would call our attention to any errors or outdated information by contacting Berlitz Publishing, 193 Morris Avenue, Springfield, NJ 07081, USA. E-mail: comments@berlitzbooks.com

First Printing: December 2010
Printed in China
ISBN 978-981-268-863-7

Publishing Director: Sheryl Olinsky Borg
Senior Editor/Project Manager: Lorraine Sova, Monica Bentley
Cover Design: Claudia Petrilli, Leighanne Tillman
Editorial: Alejandra Gritsipis, Nita M. Renfrew
Production Manager: Elizabeth Gaynor
Composition: Datagrafix, Inc.
Cover: Suitcase, Care of iStockphoto.com/edge69; Stamps, Leighanne Tillman

Contents

 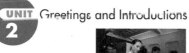

Contents

How to Use This Book

By using *5-Minute Travel Spanish* every day, you can start speaking Spanish in just minutes. The 5-Minute program introduces you to a new language and gets you ready for your trip. Take a few minutes before or after work, before you go to sleep at night or any time that feels right to work on one lesson a day. If you want, you can even do some last-minute learning on the plane or train! Just have fun while you learn; you'll be speaking Spanish in no time.

- The book is divided into 99 lessons. Each provides a bite-sized learning opportunity that you can complete in minutes.

- Each unit has 8 lessons presenting important vocabulary, phrases and other information needed while you travel.

- A review at the end of each unit provides an opportunity to test your knowledge before you move on.

- Unless otherwise noted, *5-Minute Travel Spanish* uses formal language. In everyday Spanish, the formal is usually used between adults who are not close friends or family and in professional settings. The informal is used with familiar friends and family and when addressing children

Buenos días¡

- Real-life language and activities introduce the vocabulary, phrases and grammar covered in the lessons that follow. You'll see dialogues, postcards, e-mails and other everyday correspondence in Spanish.
- You can listen to the dialogues, articles, e-mails and other presentations on the *5-Minute Travel Spanish* audio CD.

Smart Phrases

- In these lessons you'll find useful everyday phrases. You can listen to these phrases on the audio program.
- Extra Phrases enrich your knowledge and understanding of everyday Spanish. These are not practiced in the activities, but they're there for those who want to learn.

Words to Know

- Core Words are important words related to the lesson topic. In some lessons these words are divided into sub-categories. You can listen to these words on our audio program.
- Extra Words are other helpful words to know.

Smart Grammar

- Don't let the name scare you. Smart Grammar covers the basic parts of speech you'll need to know if you want to speak Spanish easily and fluently.
- From verb usage to forming questions, the 5-Minute program provides quick and easy explanations and examples for how to use these structures.

Unit Review Here you'll have a chance to practice what you've learned.

Challenge
Extend your knowledge even further with a challenge activity.

Internet Activity
- Internet activities take you to **www.berlitzbooks.com/5Mtravel**, where you can test drive your new language skills. Just look for the computer symbol.

5-Minute Travel Spanish audio
When you see this symbol , you'll know to listen to the specified track on the *5-Minute Travel Spanish* audio CD.

SMART TIP
Boxes like these are here to extend your Spanish knowledge. You'll find differences in Spanish from country to country, extra language conventions and other helpful information on how to speak better Spanish.

CULTURE TIP
Boxes like these introduce useful cultural information about Spanish-speaking countries.

SMART PRONUNCIATION
Boxes like these demonstrate specific pronunciation tools. For example, did you know that in some countries the letter *d* is pronounced with a lisp? You'll learn more as you move further along in the book.

This section is designed to make you familiar with the sounds of Spanish using our simplified phonetic transcription. You'll find the pronunciation of the Spanish letters and sounds explained below, together with their "imitated" equivalents. Simply read the pronunciation as if it were English, noting any special rules below.

The acute accent ' indicates stress, e.g. *río* <u>ree</u>·oh. Some Spanish words have more than one meaning. In these instances, the accent mark is also used to distinguish between them, e.g.: *él* (he) and *el* (the); *sí* (yes) and *si* (if).

Consonants

Letter	Approximate Pronunciation	Example	Pronunciation
b	1. as in English b	**bueno**	<u>bweh</u>·noh
	2. between vowels as in English, but softer	**bebida**	beh·<u>bee</u>·dah
c	1. before e and i like s in same	**centro**	<u>sehn</u>·troh
	2. otherwise like k in kit	**como**	<u>koh</u>·moh
g	1. before e and i, like ch in Scottish loch	**urgente**	oor·<u>khehn</u>·teh
	2. otherwise, like g in get	**ninguno**	neen·<u>goo</u>·noh
h	always silent	**hombre**	<u>ohm</u>·breh
j	like ch in Scottish loch	**bajo**	<u>bah</u>·khoh
ll	like y in yellow	**lleno**	<u>yeh</u>·noh
ñ	like ni in onion	**señor**	seh·<u>nyohr</u>
q	like k in kick	**quince**	<u>keen</u>·seh
r	trilled, especially at the beginning of a word	**río**	<u>ree</u>·oh
rr	strongly trilled	**arriba**	ah·<u>rree</u>·bah
s	1. like s in same	**sus**	soos
	2. before b, d, g, l, m, n, like s in rose	**mismo**	<u>meez</u>·moh
v	like b in bad, but softer	**viejo**	<u>beeyeh</u>·khoh
z	like s in same	**brazo**	<u>brah</u>·soh

Letters ch, d, f, k, l, m, n, p, t, w, x and y are pronounced as in English.

Vowels

Letter	Approximate Pronunciation	Example	Pronunciation
a	like the a in father	**gracias**	grah·seeyahs
e	like e in get	**esta**	ehs·tah
i	like ee in meet	**sí**	see
o	like o in rope	**dos**	dohs
u	1. like oo in food	**uno**	oo·noh
	2. silent after g and q	**que**	keh
	3. when marked ü, like we in well	**antigüedad**	ahn·tee·gweh·dahd
y	1. like y in yellow	**hoy**	oy
	2. when alone, like ee in meet	**y**	ee
	3. when preceded by an a, sounds like y + ee, with ee faintly pronounced	**hay**	aye

Below are some major consonant differences you'll hear in the Spanish spoken in Spain as opposed to most countries in Latin America.

Letter	Approximate Pronunciation	Example	Pronunciation
c	1. before e and i like th in then	**centro**	then·troh
	2. otherwise like k in kit	**como**	koh·moh
d	1. as in English	**donde**	dohn·deh
	2. between vowels and especially at the end of a word, like th in thin, but softer	**usted**	oos·teth
z	like th in thin	**brazo**	brah·thoh

In this unit you will learn:

- how to talk about different means of transportation.
- personal pronouns and the verb *ir* (to go).
- the days of the week and the months of the year.
- how to check in at the airport.

LESSON 1

¡Buen viaje!

Dialogue

Marco is talking to his colleague, Cristina, who is getting ready to go on a trip.

Marco	¿Adónde va usted de vacaciones?
Cristina	Yo voy a Barcelona.
Marco	¿Va usted en avión?
Cristina	No, voy a tomar el tren.

SMART TIPS

- The word for vacation [holiday] is *vacaciones*, and it's always plural. For example, if you want to tell someone that you are on vacation, you say *Estoy de vacaciones.*

- Did you notice that the Spanish put an inverted question mark at the beginning of a question in addition to the question mark at the end? They do the same for exclamation points, which look like ¡Vacaciones!

Activity A

Circle **T** for true and **F** for false.

1	Cristina is going on a business trip.	T / F
2	Cristina is going to Barcelona.	T / F
3	Cristina is going by plane.	T / F
4	Cristina is going by train.	T / F

Activity B

Listen to the dialogue again and fill in the missing words.

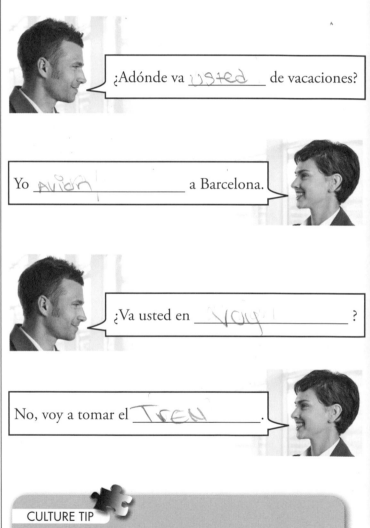

¿Adónde va ___usted___ de vacaciones?

Yo ___Avión___ a Barcelona.

¿Va usted en ___you___ ?

No, voy a tomar el ___Tren___.

CULTURE TIP

Did you know that the average worker in Spain gets only 5 days of paid vacation a year? They also work a 38.2-hour workweek, which is almost 2 ½ hours more than the rest of the European Union.

LESSON 2
Words to Know

CULTURE TIP

Are you used to taking taxis to get around town? If you want to see cities the way locals do, try taking the subway, bus, or even renting a bicycle that larger cities make available for short-term rentals. It's a great way to save money and see more of the city!

Core Words

 el avión — airplane (m)

la bici — bicycle

 el bote — boat

 el bus — bus

 el coche — car

 el crucero — cruise

 la limosina — shuttle

 el metro — subway

 el taxi — taxi

 el tren — train

SMART TIP

Did you notice that some words begin with *el* and others with *la*? These are definite articles that mean "the." Spanish is a gendered language and all nouns are either masculine (*el*) or feminine (*la*). As you progress through this book, make sure you learn the gender of each word along with the word itself.

Activity A

Match the picture in the left column with the correct Spanish word in the right column.

1 **a** el avión

2 **b** la bici

3 **c** el bote

4 **d** el coche

5 **e** el metro

Activity B

Use the words below to identify the best means of travel for each example.

> el avión   el coche   la bici   la limosina   el bote

1 traveling from New York to Barcelona _____

2 taking a guided tour down the Guadalquivir River _____

3 getting from the airport to your hotel _____

4 driving through the Valle de los Caídos _____

5 pedaling through the center of Madrid _____

Smart Phrases

Core Phrases

Ella va en bote.	She is going by boat.
Nosotros vamos en avión.	We are going by plane.
Yo voy a alquilar un coche en España.	I am going to rent a car in Spain.
Usted va en crucero.	You are going on a cruise.
¿En dónde se encuentra la parada de taxis?	Where is the taxi stand [taxi rank]?
¿Hay servicio de limosina?	Is there shuttle service?
Vosotros debéis tomar el metro.	You must take the subway.
Él va a alquilar una bici.	He is going to rent a bicycle.

SMART TIP

You may have noticed some different articles in these examples. *El* (m)/*la* (f) are definite articles and *un* (m)/*una* (f) are indefinite articles. For example, *el coche* is "the car" while *un coche* is "a car".

CULTURE TIP

If you decide to rent a car in Europe, sometimes bigger isn't always better. A smaller car will allow you to easily navigate the narrow roads of some of the larger cities and will also make parking a lot easier! Be careful, though, because most rental cars in Europe are standard, not automatic. If you need an automatic car, make sure you request one ahead of time.

Activity A

Fill in the blank using the image as a guide.

1   Ustedes van en _____.

2   ¿En dónde se encuentra la parada de _____ ?

3   Voy a alquilar un _____ en España.

4   Nosotros vamos en _____.

Activity B

How would you…

1   …ask where the taxi stand is?
_____

2   …tell someone you're going to rent a car?
_____

3   …say that she is taking a boat?
_____

4   …ask if there is shuttle service?
_____

Smart Grammar

Personal Pronouns

yo	I
tú	you (sing., inf.)
usted	you (sing., form.)
él/ella	he/she
nosotros/nosotras	we (m/f)
vosotros/vosotras	you (pl., m/f SP)
ustedes	you (pl. LA)
ellos/ellas	they (m/f)

Abbreviations

masculine	m	singular	sing.
informal	inf.	feminine	f
plural	pl.	formal	form.
Latin America	LA	Spain	SP

SMART TIP

It is important to distinguish between the informal and formal pronouns in Spanish. When speaking to friends, children and pets, use the informal *tú*. When talking to strangers or someone you've just met, use the formal *usted* until the other person says that you can use the informal *tú*.

Activity A

Fill in the blank with the correct singular pronoun.

1 (I) _____ voy de vacaciones.

2 (He) _____ va a Mallorca.

3 (She) _____ va a Madrid.

4 (You, form.) _____ va a Ginebra.

Activity B

Fill in the blanks with the correct plural personal pronoun.

1 (We) _____ vamos en coche.

2 (They) _____ van en avión.

3 (You, pl.) _____ vais en tren.

4 (They) _____ van en crucero.

SMART TIPS

- Use the masculine plural, *ellos*, if there is least one male in the group.

- The personal pronoun *uno* can mean either the number one or "one," as in "One must always be polite," *Uno debe ser amable*. It is conjugated the same as *él/ella*.

- You may have noticed that there isn't a Spanish equivalent for "it." For example, if you want to say that the airplane is big, *El avión es grande*, you can simply say *Es grande*, "it is big."

LESSON 5
La partida

The Departure

Robert is planning a trip to Spain. Here's a list of what he needs to do before he goes.

PARA HACER

comprar un boleto	buy my ticket
renovar mi pasaporte	renew my passport
hacer mis maletas	pack my bags
elegir una guía turística	choose a guide book
cambiar dólares/ libras a euros	change dollars/ pounds into euros
encontrar un hotel	find a hotel
reservar un coche de alquiler	reserve a rental car
aprender más español	learn more Spanish

SMART TIP

All of the verbs above are in the infinitive, the most basic form of a verb. In later lessons you will learn how to conjugate the three main groups of Spanish verbs, –ar, –er and –ir verbs, as well as irregular verbs.

Activity A

Fill in the missing words.

1  comprar un _____

2  hacer mis _maletas_____

3  cambiar _____ /
   _____ a _____

4  renovar mi _____

5  reservar un _____ de alquiler

Activity B

Are you going on vacation soon? Make a list of some things you need to do before you go!

PARA HACER

1. _____
2. _____
3. _____
4. _____
5. _____

LESSON 6

Words to Know

SEPTIEMBRE

VIAJE

Core Words

Los días de la semana (Days of the Week)

lunes	Monday
martes	Tuesday
miércoles	Wednesday
jueves	Thursday
viernes	Friday
sábado	Saturday
domingo	Sunday

Los meses del año (Months of the Year)

enero	January
febrero	February
marzo	March
abril	April
mayo	May
junio	June
julio	July
agosto	August
septiembre	September
octubre	October
noviembre	November
diciembre	December

Extra Words

hoy	today
mañana	tomorrow
ayer	yesterday
el día	day
la semana	week
el mes	month
el año	year

CULTURE TIP

While the week begins with Sunday on American calendars, it begins with Monday on Spanish calendars. Be especially careful if you're booking reservations online.

Activity A

Label the following numbered days of the week.

febrero

L	M	M	J	V	S	D
	1.			2.		
3.					4.	
		5.				6.
			7.			

1 _____   5 _____

2 _____   6 _____

3 _____   7 _____

4 _____

Activity B

Put the months in order from 1–12.

agosto	_____	marzo	_____
diciembre	_____	febrero	_____
abril	_____	octubre	_____
noviembre	_____	mayo	_____
julio	_____	junio	_____
enero	_____	septiembre	_____

SMART TIPS

- Days and months begin with lower-case letters in Spanish, unlike their upper-case equivalents in English.

- In Spanish, dates are abbreviated in the order day/month/year. For example, January 8, 2011 would be 8/1/2011. August 1, 2011 would be 1/8/2011.

LESSON 7

Smart Phrases

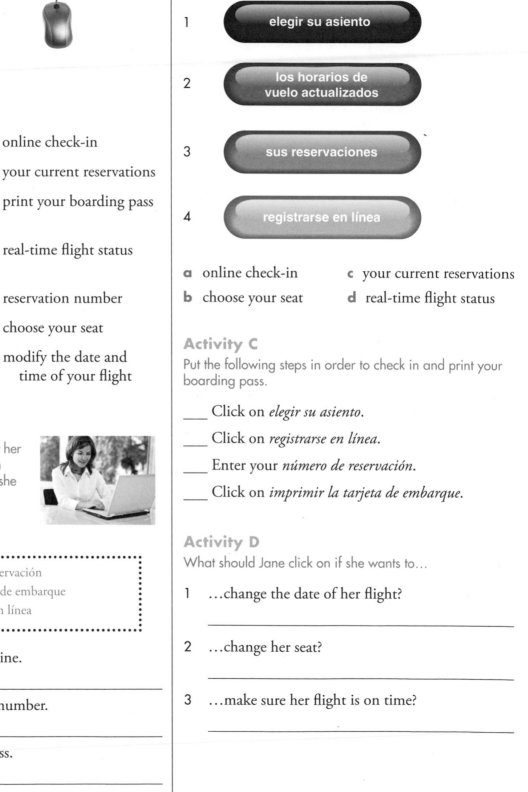

Core Phrases

registrarse en línea	online check-in
sus reservaciones	your current reservations
imprimir el boleto de embarque	print your boarding pass
los horarios de vuelo actualizados	real-time flight status
número de reservación	reservation number
elegir el asiento	choose your seat
modificar el día y la hora del vuelo	modify the date and time of your flight

Activity A

Jane has decided to check in for her flight online. Use the words from the word bank to tell her where she needs to click in order to…

> número de reservación
> imprimir el boleto de embarque
> inscribirse en línea

1 …begin checking in online.

_____

2 …enter her reservation number.

_____

3 …print her boarding pass.

_____

Activity B

Match the following links to their English equivalents.

1 **elegir su asiento**

2 **los horarios de vuelo actualizados**

3 **sus reservaciones**

4 **registrarse en línea**

a online check-in   c your current reservations
b choose your seat   d real-time flight status

Activity C

Put the following steps in order to check in and print your boarding pass.

____ Click on *elegir su asiento*.

____ Click on *registrarse en línea*.

____ Enter your *número de reservación*.

____ Click on *imprimir la tarjeta de embarque*.

Activity D

What should Jane click on if she wants to…

1 …change the date of her flight?

_____

2 …change her seat?

_____

3 …make sure her flight is on time?

_____

LESSON 8

Smart Grammar

The verb *ir* (to go)

The verb *ir* is irregular. The chart shows its conjugation in the present tense.

yo	voy	I go
tú	vas	you go
usted	va	you go
él/ella	va	he/she goes
nosotros/nosotras	vamos	we go
vosotros/vosotras	vais	you go
ustedes	van	you go
ellos/ellas	van	they go

> **SMART TIP**
>
> The verb *ir* can be used to create the future tense in Spanish. Just take one of the conjugated verbs from above and add an infinitive verb after it. For example, *Yo voy a comer* means, "I'm going to eat."

Activity A

Fill in the blank with the correct form of *ir*.

1 Nosotros _____ a España.

2 Ella _____ de vacaciones.

3 Yo _____ a hacer mis maletas.

4 Ellos _____ a tomar el tren.

5 Vosotros _____ a Madrid.

6 Tú _____ al aeropuerto.

7 Él _____ a comprar un boleto.

8 Ellas _____ en crucero.

Activity B

Answer the following questions using *sí*, "yes."

Example: ¿Vas a Madrid?
 Sí, yo voy a Madrid.

1 ¿Vamos nosotros a Barcelona?

_____

2 ¿Vais vosotros a Galicia?

_____

3 ¿Van ellos a Venezuela?

_____

4 ¿Vas tú a Mallorca?

_____

> **SMART TIP**
>
> You may have noticed that questions can be formed in Spanish by inverting the personal pronoun and the verb. For example:
>
> *Vosotros vais a Madrid.*   You go to Madrid.
>
> *¿Vais vosotros a Madrid?*   Are you going to Madrid?

Activity C

Complete the following sentences with the correct form of *ir*.

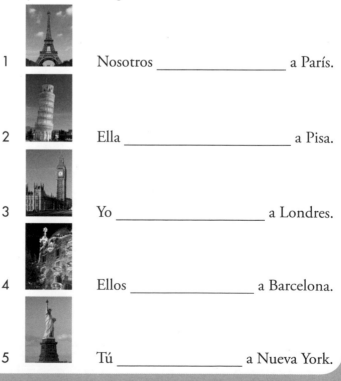

1 Nosotros _____ a París.

2 Ella _____ a Pisa.

3 Yo _____ a Londres.

4 Ellos _____ a Barcelona.

5 Tú _____ a Nueva York.

Unit 1 Review

Activity A

Label the following means of transportation.

1 _____

2 _____

3 _____

4 _____

Activity B

Listen to the dialogue from Lesson 1 and fill in the blanks below.

Marco	¿Adónde _____ de vacaciones?
Cristina	Yo _____ a Barcelona.
Marco	¿Va usted en _____ ?
Cristina	No, voy a tomar el _____ .

Activity C

Put the days of the week in order from 1–7.

____ miércoles

____ domingo

____ lunes

____ jueves

____ sábado

____ martes

____ viernes

Activity D

Complete the following table for the verb *ir*.

yo	.
	vas
usted	
él/ella	
nosotros	
	vais
ustedes	
	van

Activity E

Complete the word search to find words related to travel, days and months.

avión	bote	carro
domingo	ellas	enero
ir	lunes	maleta
miércoles	nosotros	octubre
sábado	vacaciones	

```
P  J  R  H  S  E  U  M  B  X  P  U  C  N  F
Y  M  E  U  I  N  M  A  L  E  T  A  R  C  L
G  M  L  L  L  E  C  H  W  U  R  R  E  S  U
O  S  L  R  E  R  M  Z  X  J  P  R  P  J  N
Z  R  A  E  C  O  I  J  F  V  B  R  J  K  E
A  P  S  B  R  Q  E  M  F  U  G  V  O  D  S
V  Y  Y  U  A  T  R  L  T  T  N  D  B  O  O
I  I  R  Z  B  D  C  C  M  E  O  O  F  M  C
O  W  A  S  O  L  O  T  J  S  S  M  Z  P  J
N  U  Y  Z  T  O  L  Z  X  U  O  I  Q  C  P
I  U  T  E  E  M  E  D  J  X  T  N  R  A  R
T  R  A  P  O  Z  S  A  M  Z  R  G  P  R  X
H  S  K  X  V  Z  X  D  S  L  O  O  Q  R  B
D  K  K  V  E  L  T  K  U  O  S  Y  X  O  Z
T  V  A  C  A  C  I  O  N  E  S  F  P  T  X
```

Internet Activity

Want help practicing your verb conjugations? Go to iTunes® and search for "Berlitz" to download the Berlitz verb app for your iPod touch® or iPhone®. The more you practice your verbs, the easier they become!

In this unit you will learn:
- the numbers 0–60 and time.
- how to greet others and introduce yourself.
- the verbs *ser/estar* (to be).
- how to talk about different countries, languages and nationalities.

LESSON 1
Yo me llamo…

Dialogue

Catalina has just boarded her plane to Spain and the gentleman seated next to her decides to strike up a conversation.

Jerónimo	Buenos días. Yo me llamo Jerónimo. ¿Cómo se llama usted?
Catalina	Buenos días. Yo me llamo Catalina. Encantada.
Jerónimo	Encantado. ¿Es usted americana?
Catalina	Sí, yo soy americana. ¿Es usted español?
Jerónimo	No, yo soy canario. ¿Está usted de vacaciones?
Catalina	Sí, yo estoy de vacaciones. Yo voy a Madrid.

SMART TIPS

- A very easy way to say "Nice to meet you" in Spanish if you're a man is *encantado* (m), and if you're a woman, *encantada* (f).
- Check the Spanish-English glossary on page 114 to find out how to say other nationalities.

Activity A

Circle **T** for true and **F** for false.

1 Jerónimo asks Catalina what her name is.   **T / F**
2 Catalina is happy to meet Jerónimo.   **T / F**
3 Catalina is Spanish.   **T / F**
4 Jerónimo is on vacation.   **T / F**

Activity B

Imagine you are seated next to Jerónimo. How would you respond?

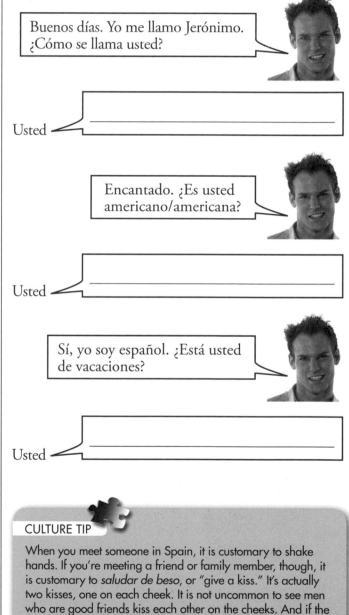

> Buenos días. Yo me llamo Jerónimo. ¿Cómo se llama usted?

Usted _____

> Encantado. ¿Es usted americano/americana?

Usted _____

> Sí, yo soy español. ¿Está usted de vacaciones?

Usted _____

CULTURE TIP

When you meet someone in Spain, it is customary to shake hands. If you're meeting a friend or family member, though, it is customary to *saludar de beso*, or "give a kiss." It's actually two kisses, one on each cheek. It is not uncommon to see men who are good friends kiss each other on the cheeks. And if the person you are meeting is very friendly, don't be surprised if he or she greets you with two kisses.

Words to Know

Note that the number 1 can be either masculine or feminine in Spanish depending on the gender of the noun. For example, *un bote* (m) is "one boat" and *una maleta* (f) is "one suitcase."

Core Words

Los números (Numbers)

cero	0	trece	13
uno	1	catorce	14
dos	2	quince	15
tres	3	dieciséis	16
cuatro	4	diecisiete	17
cinco	5	dieciocho	18
seis	6	diecinueve	19
siete	7	veinte	20
ocho	8	veintiuno	21
nueve	9	treinta	30
diez	10	cuarenta	40
once	11	cincuenta	50
doce	12	sesenta	60

Extra Words

la dirección	address
el número de teléfono	phone number
el número de vuelo	flight number

Activity A

How many of each do you see?

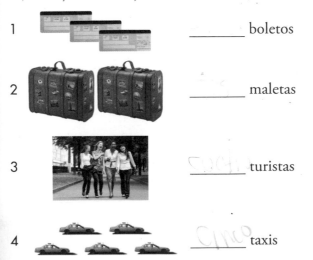

1 _____ boletos

2 _____ maletas

3 _____ turistas

4 _____ taxis

Activity B

Look at the flight departure screen and say what time the following flights are scheduled to leave.

SALIDAS			
13H40	MADRID MAD	IB 0026	A TIEMPO
13h55	ZURICH	CO 2215	A TIEMPO
14H05	BARCELONA	IB 6509	RETRASADO 30 MIN
14H15	GINEBRA	SA 1550	A TIEMPO
14H30	LONDRES LHR	BA 3022	A TIEMPO
14H40	NIZA	AF 0045	A TIEMPO

1 cero cero cuarenta y cinco _____

2 sesenta y cinco cero nueve _____

3 treinta veintidós _____

4 veintidós quince _____

Activity C

Listen to the phone numbers and write them down.

1 _____

2 _____

3 _____

When the Spanish say phone numbers they read them in groups of three and two. Phone numbers in Spain begin with a prefix according to the geographical area, similar to the area codes in the U.S. Different prefixes also apply to cell phones, depending on the area, as well as the service carrier.

LESSON 3
Smart Phrases

Core Phrases

Buenos días.	Hello.
Buenas noches.	Good evening.
Que tenga una buena noche.	Good night.
¿Cómo se llama usted?	What's your name?
Yo me llamo _____.	My name is _____.
¿Cómo está usted?	How are you?
Yo estoy bien, gracias.	I'm fine, thanks.
¿De dónde es usted?	Where are you from?
Adiós.	Goodbye.

Extra Phrases

¡Hola!	Hi!
¿Cómo vas?	How's it going?
Voy bien.	I'm fine.
¡Nos vemos!	See you soon!

SMART TIPS

- Remember that there are different levels of formality in Spanish. For example, you would say *Hola, ¿cómo vas?* to a friend, but *Buenos días, ¿cómo está usted?* to a stranger.

- There is no way to say "Good morning" in Spanish; just say *¡Buenos días!*

Activity A

Answer the following questions.

1   ¿Cómo está usted?

_____

2   ¿Cómo se llama?

_____

3   ¿De dónde viene usted?

_____

Activity B

What would these people say to each other?

1

2

3

4

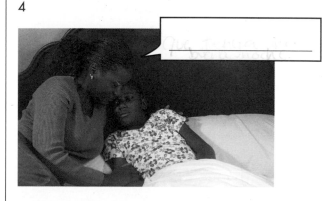

LESSON 4
Smart Grammar

The verbs *ser* and *estar* (to be)

Spanish uses two different verbs for "to be": *ser* and *estar*. When you "are" something, use *ser*. For example, *Yo soy maestra*, "I am a teacher."

	ser	to be
yo	soy	I am
tú	eres	you are
usted	es	you are
él/ella	es	he/she is
nosotros/nosotras	somos	we are
vosotros/vosotras	sois	you are
ustedes	son	you are
ellos/ellas	son	they are

When you are physically inside of a vehicle or in a place (car, train, airplane, house, etc.) use *estar*. For example, *Yo estoy en el coche*, "I am in the car."

	estar	to be
yo	estoy	I am
tú	estás	you are
usted	está	you are
él/ella	está	he/she is
nosotros/nosotras	estamos	we are
vosotros/vosotras	estáis	you are
ustedes	están	you are
ellos/ellas	están	they are

Activity A

Fill in the blanks with the correct form of *ser* or *estar*.

1 Catalina _____ americana.

2 Jesús y Jerónimo _____ españoles.

3 Nosotros _____ de vacaciones.

4 Ellos _____ en el avión.

Activity B

Answer the following questions in the affirmative.

1 ¿Está usted de vacaciones?

_____

2 ¿Es español Jerónimo?

_____

3 ¿Son americanas Catalina y Julia?

_____

4 ¿Están ellos en el tren?

_____

5 ¿Estás tú en el bus?

_____

Activity C

Complete the verb chart with the present forms of *ser* and *estar*.

yo		
tú		
usted		
él/ella		
nosotros/nosotras		
vosotros/vosotras		
ustedes		
ellos/ellas		

Your Turn

Do you know any adjectives in Spanish that would complete the statement? Use a bilingual dictionary or the glossary for help.

Yo soy _____.

LESSON 5

¿A qué hora es la salida del tren?

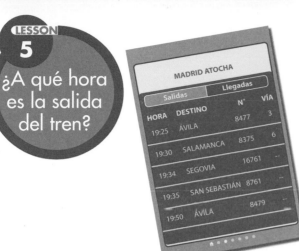

MADRID ATOCHA

	Salidas	Llegadas		
HORA	DESTINO		N°	VÍA
19:25	ÁVILA		8477	3
19:30	SALAMANCA		8375	6
19:34	SEGOVIA		16761	--
19:35	SAN SEBASTIÁN		8761	--
19:50	ÁVILA		8479	--

CULTURE TIP

The Spanish often use a 24-hour clock when writing, so there is no AM or PM. When speaking they often use the 12-hour clock. To indicate AM or PM, they might say *de la madrugada*, "before dawn," *de la mañana* "in the morning," *de la tarde* "in the afternoon," and *de la noche* "in the evening." Be extra careful when buying tickets or checking bus schedules!

Dialogue

Now that you know numbers, let's talk about time. Listen to the conversation between Stephanie and the train conductor.

Perdone. ¿A qué hora es el próximo tren a Segovia?

El próximo tren es a las diecinueve veinticinco.

¿Y el siguiente tren?

El siguiente tren es a las diecinueve cincuenta.

SMART TIP

El próximo tren means "the next train," while *el siguiente tren* means "the following train."

Activity A

Listen to the questions and answer them based on the train schedule at left.

1 _____
2 _____
3 _____
4 _____

SMART TIPS

- "A quarter after" is *y cuarto*. For example, *6:15* is *seis y cuarto*.
- "A quarter to" is *menos cuarto*. For example, *7:45* is *ocho menos cuarto*.
- "Half past" is *treinta* or *y media*. For example, *18:30* is *dieciocho treinta* or *seis y media*.
- "Noon" is *mediodía* and "midnight" is *medianoche*.

Activity B

Listen to the times said by the conductor and write which train leaves at each time.

1 _____
2 _____
3 _____
4 _____

MADRID CHAMARTÍN

	Salidas	Llegadas		
HORA	DESTINO		N°	VÍA
18:25	BARCELONA		3127	19
18:30	BARCELONA		13119	22
18:33	BILBAO		850053	--
18:45	MÁLAGA		3353	--
18:50	SEVILLA		3131	--

Core Words

Bandera (Flag)	País (Country)	Nacionalidad (Nationality)	Idioma (Language)
	Alemania	alemán/alemana (m/f)	alemán
	Australia	australiano/australiana (m/f)	inglés
	España	español/española (m/f)	español
	Los Estados Unidos	americano/americana (m/f)	inglés
	Francia	francés/francesa (m/f)	francés
	Inglaterra	inglés/inglesa (m/f)	inglés
	Italia	italiano/italiana (m/f)	italiano

SMART TIP

Note that *la nacionalidad*, the nationality, and *el idioma*, the language, aren't capitalized in Spanish like they are in English. For example:

Ella es española. She is Spanish.
Yo hablo español. I speak Spanish.

Activity A

Match each country with its flag.

1   Los Estados Unidos   **a** 
2   Italia   **b** 
3   Inglaterra   **c** 
4   España   **d** 
5   Francia   **e** 
6   Alemania   **f**

SMART TIP

Check page 114 in the glossary to learn more countries and nationalities.

Activity B

Write the language associated with each country below. Remember not to capitalize it!

1   España _____

2   Alemania _____

3   Los Estados Unidos _____

4   Italia _____

Activity C

Listen to the sentences describing the people below and label them from 1–4.

_____

_____

_____

_____

Smart Phrases

Why Travel?

Estamos de vacaciones.	We are on vacation.
Estoy de viaje de nogocios.	I am on a business trip.
Él va a visitar a su familia.	He is going to visit his family.
Ellas van a hacer montañismo en Córcega.	They are going hiking in Corsica.
Ellos van a esquiar a los Alpes.	They are going skiing in the Alps.
Vosotros vais a aprender español en Madrid.	You are going to learn Spanish in Madrid.
Ella va a hacer *surfing* en Canarias.	She is going surfing in the Canary Islands.

Activity A

Number the following travel ideas from 1–5 where 1 is your favorite and 5 is your least favorite.

_____ de negocios

_____ esquiar en los Alpes

_____ aprender español en Madrid

_____ visitar a su familia

_____ hacer montañismo en Córcega

Activity B

Say why the following people are travelling.

1 _____

2 _____

3 _____

4 _____

5 _____

> **SMART TIP**
>
> In Spanish, when you use the verb *visitar* to talk about visiting places and monuments, the place follows the verb: *Nosotros vamos a visitar el Escorial*, "We are going to visit El Escorial." When you talk about visiting people, the verb *visitar* is followed by the preposition *a*: *Yo voy a visitar a mi familia*, "I'm going to visit my family."

Masculine and Feminine

As you learned in Unit 1, all nouns have a gender in Spanish. Here are some hints to help you identify the genders of different nouns.

- Almost all words that end in –o and –e are masculine. For example:

el bote	boat
el castillo	castle
el coche	car
el peaje	toll booth
el piso	floor
el viaje	trip

- Almost all words that end in –a and –ión are feminine. For example:

la bicicleta	bicycle
la billetera	wallet
la estación	station
las instrucciones	directions
la limosina	shuttle
la pregunta	question

SMART TIPS

- The definite article *los* is used for masculine plural nouns. The definite article *las* is used for feminine plural nouns. For example, *Las bicicletas son rápidas,* "The bicycles are fast," and *Los castillos son hermosos,* "The castles are beautiful."

- Plural words end in –*s* or –*es* in Spanish. Words that end in a vowel add an –*s* in the plural: *la billetera* (wallet)/ *las billeteras* (wallets). Words that end in a consonant add –*es* in the plural: *la estación* (station)/*las estaciones* (stations). There are some exceptions to these rules and you will learn them on a case-by-case basis.

Activity A

Identify the following nouns. Don't forget to put the definite article *el/la,* or *los/las*!

1 _____

2 _____

3 _____

4 _____

SMART TIPS

- Note that countries are masculine and feminine. For example, *Francia, España, Colombia* and *Venezuela* are feminine, and *Ecuador, Brazil* and *Portugal* are masculine.

- To say that you are going to a country or city, use the preposition *a.*

Yo voy a España.	I'm going to France.
Usted va a los Estados Unidos	You're going to the United States.
Ella va a Madrid.	She's going to Madrid.
Nosotros vamos a Ginebra.	We're going to Geneva.

Activity B

Give the correct gender for each country: *m* for *masculino* and *f* for *femenino.*

1 España _____

2 Portugal _____

3 Suiza _____

4 Ecuador _____

5 Inglaterra _____

Activity A
Circle the highest number in each group.

sesenta y dos	dos	diecisiete
cincuenta y tres	cinco	diecinueve
diecinueve	once	dieciséis

Activity B
Say the nationality and language spoken by the following people.

1 Yo soy _____

   y hablo _____.

2 Yo soy _____

   y hablo _____.

3 Yo soy _____

   y hablo _____.

Activity C
Practice saying the following phone numbers out loud.

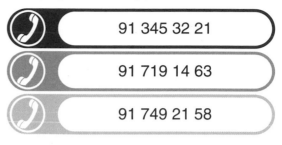

91 345 32 21

91 719 14 63

91 749 21 58

Activity D
See if you can understand when the next train leaves.

El próximo tren sale a…

1 _____   3 _____

2 _____   4 _____

Activity E
Write the definite article el/la or los/las before each noun.

1 _____ torta

2 _____ billetera

3 _____ navegación

4 _____ instrucciones

5 _____ peaje

Challenge
List five different countries along with their nationalities and the languages spoken.

Internet Activity
Go to **www.berlitzbooks.com/5Mtravel** to find a list of different countries around the world where you can practice your Spanish. Spanish is an official language in more than 23 countries!

Unit 3 Arrival

In this unit you will learn:
- **how to find your way through the airport and go through customs.**
- **the verb _tener_ (to have).**
- **how to get from the airport to your hotel.**
- **how to navigate public transportation.**

LESSON 1

¡Bienvenido!

Margaret just arrived in Spain for vacation. Here are her passport and ticket.

Puerta / Gate C3	Asiento / Seat 19B	Nombre del pasajero / Name of passenger SMITH / MARGARET De / From NEWARK EWR A / To Madrid MAD

Número de vuelo / Flight 2083	Fecha 23 MAR 2010

Salida / Departure 21H00

Activity A

The airline seems to have misplaced one of Margaret's suitcases. Help her fill out the following Lost Luggage form using the information from her passport and ticket stub.

DECLARACIÓN DE PÉRDIDA DE EQUIPAJE

Apellido : _____

Nombre : _____

Nacionalidad : _____

Fecha de nacimiento : _____

Fecha del vuelo : _____

Número del vuelo : _____

SMART TIP

Note that in Spanish _nombre_ means "given name" when filling out a form, and _apellido_ means "surname." If you have to fill out any forms in Spanish, make sure that you put your first name under _Nombre_ and your last name under _Apellido_.

Activity B

Match the Spanish word to the English word.

1	el apellido	a	first name
2	la fecha de nacimiento	b	last name
3	el nombre	c	gate
4	el lugar de nacimiento	d	date of birth
5	la puerta	e	place of birth

LESSON 2
Words to Know

Core Words

la aduana	customs
el control de pasaportes	passport control
declarar	to declare
los efectos personales	personal belongings
los impuestos de aduana	customs duty
las llegadas	arrivals
el pasaporte	passport
el retiro de equipaje	baggage claim
la salida	exit
la terminal	terminal
el transporte público	public transportation
la visa	visa

Extra Words

el carrito para equipaje	baggage cart
la escala	stopover
el oficial de aduana	customs officer

Activity A

Listen to the words and numbers on the CD and label the following images 1–5.

_____

___3___

_____

___5___

_____

Activity B

Imagine that you just arrived at the airport. Label the following steps from 1–5, where 1 is the first thing you have to do.

_____ pasar la aduana

_____ llegar a la terminal

_____ buscar la salida

_____ llegar al retiro de equipaje

_____ pasar el control de pasaportes

CULTURE TIP

If you have a long layover and want to leave your luggage, some airports and train stations have luggage storage options or lockers called *consigna de equipaje*. Just make sure you check your options before you go!

Activity C

Read the clues and complete the crossword puzzle.

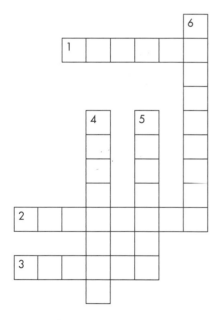

Across

1 not arrival

2 your luggage

3 customs

Down

4 where you find all the gates

5 arrival

6 document needed in order to travel

Core Phrases

¿Tiene algo que declarar?	Do you have anything to declare?
No tengo nada que declarar.	I have nothing to declare.
¿Cuánto tiempo va a estar en España?	How long will you stay in Spain?
Voy a estar dos días/semanas.	I'm going to stay for two days/weeks.
¿Cuál es el propósito de su viaje?	What is the purpose of your trip?
Estoy de vacaciones/ viaje de negocios.	I am on vacation/business.

Extra Phrases

Yo solamente estoy de paso.	I am just passing through.
Yo voy a declarar dos botellas de champaña.	I want to declare two bottles of champagne.
Abra esta maleta por favor.	Please open this suitcase.

> **SMART TIP**
>
> In order to say "this/these" in Spanish, use the words *este/ esta* (m/f) and *estos/estas* (m/f, pl.). For example, "this ticket" is *este boleto* and "these cars" is *estos carros*.

Activity A

Choose the best answer for each question.

1 ¿Tienen ustedes algo que declarar?
 a No, yo estoy de viaje de negocios.
 b No, yo no tengo nada que declarar.

2 ¿Cuánto tiempo van a estar ustedes en España?
 a Yo voy a estar tres semanas.
 b Son dos horas.

3 ¿Cuál es el motivo de su viaje?
 a Yo voy a visitar a mi familia.
 b Yo soy canadiense.

4 ¿No tienen algo que declarar?
 a Sí, yo estoy de vacaciones.
 b Sí, yo voy a declarar cuatro botellas de coñac.

Activity B

Insert the correct demonstrative pronoun (*este, esta, estos* or *estas*) below.

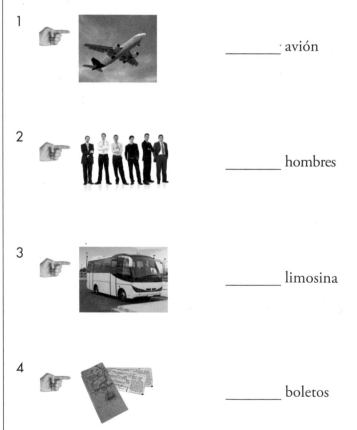

1 _____ avión

2 _____ hombres

3 _____ limosina

4 _____ boletos

The verb *tener* (to have)

The verb *tener* is irregular. The chart shows its conjugation in the present tense.

yo	tengo	I have
tú	tienes	you have
usted	tiene	you have
él/ella	tiene	he/she has
nosotros/nosotras	tenemos	we have
vosotros/vosotras	tenéis	you have
ustedes	tienen	you have
ellos/ellas	tienen	they have

SMART TIP

The Spanish verb *haber* also means "to have." A good expression to learn is *hay*, which means "there is/there are." For example, *Hay un taxi en la calle* means "There is a taxi in the street." Likewise, *Hay dos taxis en la calle* means "There are two taxis in the street." You can also say, *Hay un parque en este barrio*, "There is a park in this neighborhood," instead of *Este barrio tiene un parque*, "This neighborhood has a park."

Activity A

Fill in the blanks with the correct form of *tener*.

1 Nosotros _____ un coche de alquiler.

2 Yo _____ dos maletas.

3 Juan _____ un pasaporte español.

4 Raquel y Ana _____ reservaciones para el hotel.

SMART TIP

The verb *tener* can be used to express a variety of feelings in Spanish.

Examples

Yo tengo sed.	I'm thirsty.
Él tiene hambre.	He's hungry.
Nosotros tenemos miedo.	We're afraid.
Ellos tienen sueño.	They're sleepy.
Tú tienes frío.	You're cold.
Ellos tienen calor.	They're hot.

Activity B

Listen to the audio and match each statement with the correct picture.

1 _____   2 _____

3 _____   4 _____

5 _____

¡Taxi!

Dialogue

Frank has just arrived in Madrid and is taking a taxi to his hotel. Follow along with the dialogue while listening to the audio.

Chauffeur	Buenos días. ¿A dónde van ustedes?
Frank	Buenos días. Nosotros vamos al hotel El Prado.
Chauffeur	¿Cuál es la dirección?
Frank	Prado 11. ¿Puedo pagarle con tarjeta de crédito?
Chauffeur	Lo siento, pero tiene que pagar en efectivo.
Frank	¿Me puede dar un recibo por favor?

Activity A

What really happened to Frank? Circle **T** for True and **F** for False.

1	Frank toma el bus.	**T / F**
2	Frank va al hotel El Prado.	**T / F**
3	Él va a pagar con una tarjeta de crédito.	**T / F**
4	Frank pide un recibo.	**T / F**

SMART TIP

There are a few different ways of saying "receipt" in Spanish. For example, in a taxi, you ask for *un recibo*, at a hotel you ask for *una factura*, and at a store, you ask for *una boleta de venta*.

Activity B

Pretend you are Frank and answer the taxi driver's questions.

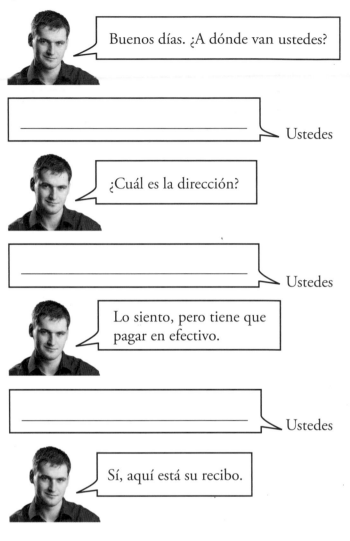

Buenos días. ¿A dónde van ustedes?

_____ Ustedes

¿Cuál es la dirección?

_____ Ustedes

Lo siento, pero tiene que pagar en efectivo.

_____ Ustedes

Sí, aquí está su recibo.

Activity C

What does the taxi driver say to you if…

1 …he wants to know the address of the hotel?

_____

2 …he is sorry?

_____

3 …you can only pay in cash?

_____

LESSON 6 — Words to Know

Using a ticket machine

Here are the words you need to know to purchase tickets from an automatic ticket machine in the *métro*.

cancelar	cancel
validación	OK/accept
pagar	pay
comprar billetes	buy tickets
Haga su selección en la pantalla y presione validar.	Make your selection on the screen, then press OK.
billete sencillo	single ticket
tarifa	full price
abono de 10 viajes	booklet of 10 tickets
Elija la cantidad deseada.	Select desired number of tickets.
¿Desea un recibo?	Would you like a receipt?
Para pagar, introduzca monedas, billetes o su tarjeta de crédito.	To pay, insert coins, bills or your credit card.
total	total due
Esta máquina devuelve cambio.	This machine returns change.

SMART TIPS

- *Validar* or *validación* can mean "to press OK" or "to validate one's ticket" before getting on the subway.
- In some cities like *Sevilla*, you have to validate your ticket when entering and exiting a train station. In this case, a minimum will be charged when entering, and the rest of the fare will be applied as you exit. Not sure about what to do? Just observe the locals and do as they do.

Activity A

For each image, would you select A or B if you wanted to…

1   …buy a subway ticket?

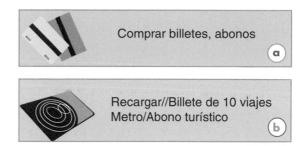

Comprar billetes, abonos (a)

Recargar//Billete de 10 viajes Metro/Abono turístico (b)

2   …select "Cancel"?

VALIDAR (a)   CANCELAR (b)

3   …buy a booklet of tickets?

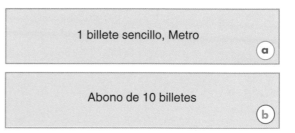

1 billete sencillo, Metro (a)

Abono de 10 billetes (b)

Activity B

Put the steps in the correct order to buy a ticket.

___ Validar.

___ Elija "billete sencillo."

___ Elija "comprar billetes."

___ Pagar.

CULTURE TIP

Not all non-Spanish credit cards work in *metro* machines. It's easiest to pay with change, *monedas*, or bills, *billetes*. If you need to pay with a credit card, you might have to go to a ticket counter.

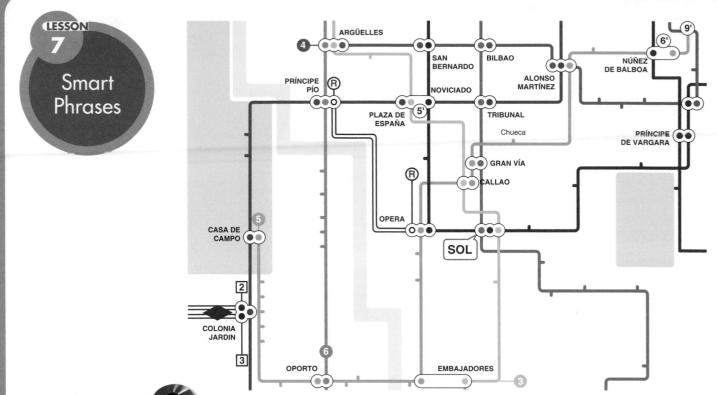

LESSON 7
Smart Phrases

Using the *métro* 💿

Validar el billete.	Validate your ticket.
Tome el metro, línea ____.	Take subway line ____.
Tome la línea 5, con dirección a Casa de Campo.	Take line 5 toward Casa de Campo.
Suba en ____.	Get on at ____.
Baje en ____.	Get off at ____.
Cambie en ____.	Change at ____.
Continúe ____ estaciones.	Go ____ stops.
Vaya hasta la última estación.	Go to the last stop.

SMART TIPS

- When someone tells you to get off at the first, second, third, etc. "stop" (*estación*), he/she uses an ordinal number. The first ten ordinal numbers in Spanish are: *primero(a), segundo(a), tercero(a), cuarto(a), quinto(a), sexto(a), séptimo(a), octavo(a), noveno(a), décimo(a).*

- Metro stops are often abbreviated as M.

Activity A

Using the subway map, follow the directions to find the final destination.

1   Suba en Plaza de España.

2   Tome la línea 3, con dirección a Embajadores.

3   Cambie en Callao.

4   Tome la línea 5, con dirección a Casa de Campo.

5   Vaya hasta la última estación.

¿En dónde estoy?   Where am I?

_____

Activity B 💿

Listen to the directions and find the final destination using the subway map.

1   ¿En dónde estoy?

_____

2   ¿En dónde estoy?

_____

LESSON 8

Smart Grammar

Definite/Indefinite Articles

You have already learned the definite articles *el/la* and *los/las*. Now you will learn the indefinite articles *un/una* and *unos/unas*. While definite articles refer to something specific (the plane, the pilots), indefinite articles are more general (a plane, some pilots.) Take a look at the following chart of definite and indefinite articles.

	Definite	Indefinite
m sing.	el	un
f sing.	la	una
m pl.	los	unos
f pl.	las	unas

Example 1

Yo tengo el billete.   I have the ticket.

Example 2

Yo tengo un billete.   I have a ticket.

Example 1 refers to a specific ticket, while Example 2 refers to an unspecified ticket.

SMART TIP

With the verb *amar*, "to love," always use definite articles to talk about things you love in general. You will learn how to conjugate this verb in the next Unit.

Yo amo los libros.   I love books.
Yo amo los niños.   I love children.

Activity A

Insert the correct definite article to refer to the pictures below.

1 _____ mujer

2 _____ avión

3 _____ equipaje de mano

Activity B

Insert the correct indefinite article to refer to the pictures below.

1 _____ maleta

2 _____ hombre

3 _____ coches

Activity C

Fill in the blanks with the correct definite or indefinite article.

1 ¡Amo _____ ciudades grandes!

2 Voy a tomar _____ metro.

3 Nosotros vamos a _____ ciudad.

4 _____ hombres y _____ mujeres están en el aeropuerto.

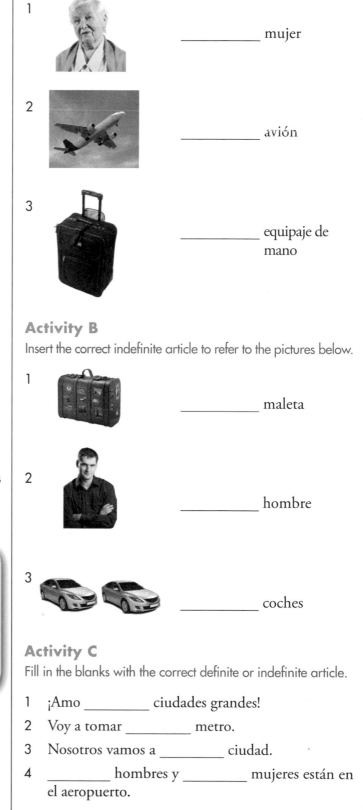

Unit 3 Review

Activity A
Fill out the top of this Customs Declaration using your information.

> **DECLARACIÓN DE ADUANA**
>
> Apellido ....
>
> Nombre ....
>
> Nacionalidad ....
>
> Fecha de nacimiento ....
>
> Lugar de nacimiento ....

Activity B
How would you ask…

1   …for a receipt in a taxi?

_____

2   …if you can pay by credit card?

_____

3   …what the address is?

_____

> **Challenge**
> Can you think of 5 different expressions that use the verb *tener*? Here's a hint: Don't be afraid!
>
> _____
> _____
> _____
> _____
> _____

Activity C
Identify the items using the correct indefinite article.

1   _____

2   _____

3   _____

Activity D
Use the subway map from Lesson 7 to explain how to get…

1   …from Sol to Chueca.

_____
_____
_____

2   …from Callao to Príncipe Pío.

_____
_____
_____

Internet Activity

Go online to **www.berlitzbooks.com/5Mtravel** where you will find the maps of some of Spain's largest *metros*. Practice saying how to get from one stop to another. For example, can you say how to get from *Santa Justa* to *Ronda de Triana* on the Seville *metro*? From *Pont d'Esplugues* to *Sagrada Familia* on the Barcelona *metro*?

Unit 4 Checking In

In this unit you will learn:

- **how to check into a hotel room.**
- **negations and how to conjugate –ar verbs.**
- **adjectives to describe your room.**
- **questions you might need to ask at the hotel.**

LESSON

1

En el hotel

Dialogue

Sr. Blanco has just arrived at the Hotel Triana. Listen to and follow along with the dialogue.

El empleado   Buenos días y bienvenido al Hotel Triana.

Sr. Blanco   Tengo una reserva a nombre de Carlos Blanco.

El empleado   Sí, usted tiene una habitación del doce al diecinueve de agosto para dos personas.

Sr. Blanco   ¿Cuánto es por noche?

El empleado   Son sesenta y cinco euros la noche.

SMART TIPS

- The word *bienvenido* is used to welcome someone. For example, *Bienvenido a España* means "Welcome to Spain."

- The abbreviation *Sr.* is short for *Señor*, or "Mr." You may also see *Sra.*, which is short for *Señora*, or "Mrs.," and *Srta.*, which is short for *Señorita* or "Miss."

Activity A

Answer the following questions.

1   For how long is Sr. Blanco staying at the Hotel Triana? _____

2   How many people are staying in the room?

_____

3   How much does the room cost per night?

_____

Activity B

Read the dialogue again and look for cognates, or words that look similar in Spanish and English.

1   _____

2   _____

3   _____

4   _____

Activity C

Answer the following questions.

1   Imagine that you are checking into a hotel. How would you present yourself?

_____

2   How would you ask how much the room is per night?

_____

LESSON 2

Words to Know

Core Words

el aire acondicionado	air conditioning
la bañera	tub
el baño completo	bathroom (with tub or shower)
la cama	bed
conexión a Internet de alta velocidad	high-speed Internet access
el cuarto de baño	bathroom (without tub or shower)
la ducha	shower
el escritorio	desk
la habitación	room
el piso	floor
la planta baja	ground floor
la tele	television
el teléfono	telephone

Extra Words

la cama doble	double bed
la cama individual	single bed
la silla	chair

CULTURE TIP

In Spain, the ground floor is labeled 0 and called the *planta baja*. The second floor is labeled 1 and called the *primer piso*. Therefore, a Spanish 5th floor (*quinto piso*) is actually an American 6th floor. If you are renting an apartment in Spain and it says "5th-floor walkup," just know that you'll be walking up six flights of stairs!

Activity A

Read the hotel confirmation and circle **T** for true or **F** for false.

Confirmación de reserva	
Hotel San Pedro ✩ ✩ ✩ ✩	• Habitación en la planta baja • Baño completo • Cama doble • Aire acondicionado • Escritorio • Conexión a Internet alta velocidad

1. The hotel room is on the second floor.   T /**F**
2. There is a bathroom with a shower.   **T**/ F
3. There is air conditioning.   **T**/ F
4. There is high-speed Internet.   **T**/ F
5. There is a single bed.   T /**F**

SMART TIP

Con means "with" and *sin* means "without." For example, *una habitación con cama doble* means "a room with a double bed."

Activity B

Listen to the words and label the following images 1–4.

a

b

_____

_____

c

d

_____

_____

Core Phrases

¿Puede usted recomendarme un hotel?	Can you recommend a hotel?
Hice una reserva…	I made a reservation…
por teléfono	on the phone
por Internet	on the Internet
con una agencia de viajes	with a travel agency
¿Tiene usted una habitación…?	Do you have a room…?
para una persona/ dos personas	for one person/ two people
con baño completo	with a bathroom
con aire acondicionado	with air conditioning
fumador/no fumador	that is smoking/ non-smoking
accessible a personas de movilidad reducida	that is handicapped accessible
¿Cuánto es por noche?	How much is it a night?
Necesito…	I need…
una cama adicional	an extra bed
una cuna	a crib
una cama doble	a double bed

> **SMART TIP**
>
> You already know how to ask questions using inversion. Another option is to add question marks and change the inflection of a declarative sentence to turn it into a question. For example: "Am I going to the hotel?" *¿Yo voy al hotel?* or "Does the room have a double bed?" *¿La habitación tiene una cama doble?*

Activity A
What would you say if…

1 …you needed an extra bed?

_____

2 …you made a reservation on the Internet?

_____

3 …you wanted to know if the hotel has a non-smoking room?

_____

4 …you wanted a room for two people, with a bathroom?

_____

Activity B
Match the questions to the answers that you hear from the hotel clerks. Label the questions 1–4.

_____ ¿Tiene una habitación con aire acondicionado?

_____ ¿Cuánto es por noche?

_____ ¿Tiene una habitación para dos personas?

_____ ¿Tiene usted una habitación no fumador?

Your Turn
Imagine that you're planning your trip to Spain and you need to book a hotel room. Practice saying out loud what kind of room you need, and make sure to find out how much it costs!

LESSON 4

Smart Grammar

Negations

Negations are formed in Spanish using the word *no* before the conjugated verb. For example:

Hay una cama.
There is a bed.

No hay televisión.
There is no television.

Carlos es español.
Carlos is Spanish.

Carlos no es italiano.
Carlos is not Italian.

Este coche funciona.
This car works.

Este coche no funciona.
This car doesn't work.

Activity A

Rewrite each sentence in the negative.

1   La habitación está en la planta baja.

   _____

2   Hay cuarto de baño en la habitación.

   _____

3   La ducha funciona.

   _____

4   Necesito una cuna.

   _____

Activity B

Answer each question in the negative.

1   ¿Es francés Harry?

   _____

2   ¿Funciona el teléfono?

   _____

3   ¿Hay una bañera?

   _____

4   ¿Habla español Peter?

   _____

CULTURE TIP

Often in spoken and written Spanish the indefinite article is eliminated. For example, you may hear someone ask *¿Hay televisión en la habitación?* "Is there a television in the room?"

SMART TIP

The verb *funcionar* can be used to say if something works or not. For example, if the Internet is not working in your hotel room, you can say *El Internet no funciona*.

Mi habitación

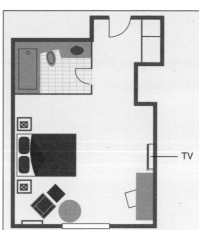

My room

Lori has just checked into her hotel room. Here is a description of her *habitación*.

Esta es mi habitación. Es grande. La cama es grande y muy cómoda. Hay una televisión. Hay una bañera en el cuarto de baño.

Adjectives

grande	big
pequeño/pequeña	small (m/f)
limpio/limpia	clean (m/f)
sucio/sucia	dirty (m/f)
cómodo/cómoda	comfortable (m/f)

SMART TIP

Adjectives, like articles, must agree with the nouns they describe. For example, *La cama es pequeña* (The room is small) and *Las habitaciones son pequeñas* (The rooms are small).

Activity A

Answer the questions about the hotel room.

1 ¿La cama es pequeña?

_____

2 ¿Hay una televisión?

_____

3 ¿Hay un escritorio y una silla?

_____

SMART TIP

If you want to talk about your hotel room, you'll need to learn the possessive adjectives. Like other adjectives, they agree with the noun that follows them (that is, with the thing that is possessed and not the possessor). This chart will help you:

	m/f sing.	m/f pl.
my	mi	mis
your	tu	tus
his/her/its	su	sus
our	nuestro/nuestra	nuestros/nuestras
your	vuestro/vuestra	vuestros/vuestras
your	su	sus
their	su	sus

Activity B

Fill in the blanks with the correct possessive adjective.

1 _____ cuarto de baño   (my)
   es muy pequeño.

2 _____ ducha no   (their)
   funciona.

3 _____ cama es cómoda.   (his/her)

4 _____ habitaciones no   (your pl.)
   son grandes.

Core Words

la almohada	pillow
el ascensor	elevator [lift]
el champú	shampoo
la escalera	staircase
el jabón	soap
el lavabo	sink
la llave	key
la manta	blanket
el papel higiénico	toilet paper
la sábana	sheet
la toalla	towel

Extra Words

la cafetera	coffee maker
la plancha	iron
la secadora de pelo	hairdryer

Activity A

Listen to the words and circle each picture that the speaker says. At the end, there should be one picture that isn't circled.

Write the Spanish word of the one picture left. _____

Activity B
¡Qué desastre!

What a disaster! Thomas and Kathleen have just checked into their room and so many things are missing. Use the pictures below to say what is missing.

1   No hay _____.

2   No hay _____.

3   No hay _____.

4   No hay _____.

SMART TIP

If you need more of something, say *Necesito más…* For example, if you need more towels, say *Necesito más toallas.*

Activity C

Complete the word webs with objects that belong in either *la habitación* or *el cuarto de baño*.

la habitación		*el cuarto de baño*	

LESSON 7

Smart Phrases

Core Phrases

No molestar.	Do not disturb.
¿Me puede dar unas toallas limpias?	Can I have some clean towels?
¿Me podría despertar a la(s) _____?	Can I get a wake-up call at _____?
¿Me podría recomendar un buen restaurante?	Could you recommend a good restaurant?
¿Me podría llamar un taxi?	Could you call me a taxi?
¿A qué hora debo desocupar la habitación?	What time is check-out?
¿Tiene un servicio de lavandería?	Do you have laundry service?
¿Podría arreglar la habitación?	Can you have my room cleaned?
Dejé mi llave en la habitación.	I left my key in the room.

Activity A

What do you say if you want...

1 ...a wake-up call at 7:00AM?

_____

2 ...the hotel to call you a taxi?

_____

3 ...to know what time check-out is?

_____

Activity B

Listen to the questions and label the photos 1–4 after deciding who is speaking.

ⓐ

ⓑ

_____ _____

ⓒ

ⓓ

_____ _____

Activity C

Match the Spanish expressions with their English equivalents.

1 ¿Me podría llamar un taxi?

2 Dejé mi llave en la habitación.

3 ¿Tiene un servicio de lavandería?

4 No molestar.

a Do not disturb.

b Could you call me a taxi?

c I left my key in the room.

d Do you have laundry service?

LESSON 8

Smart Grammar

Regular –ar verbs

Regular verbs in Spanish end in either –ar, –er, or –ir. There are also many irregular verbs that you will learn and have already learned, such as ir, ser, and tener. In this lesson you will learn how to conjugate regular –ar verbs.

To begin, remove the –ar ending, and then add the following endings:

	visitar	**to visit**
yo	visit**o**	I visit
tú	visit**as**	you visit
usted	visit**a**	you visit
él/ella	visit**a**	he/she visits
nosotros/nosotras	visit**amos**	we visit
vosotros/vosotras	visit**áis**	you visit
ustedes	visit**an**	you visit
ellos/ellas	visit**an**	they visit

Here are some regular –ar verbs:

amar	to love
bailar	to dance
buscar	to look for
escuchar	to listen to
estudiar	to study
gastar	to spend (money)
hablar	to speak
llegar	to arrive
pagar	to pay
preguntar	to ask (for)
trabajar	to work
viajar	to travel

Activity A

Conjugate the verb *hablar*, to speak.

yo	_____
tú	_____
usted	_____
él/ella	_____
nosotros/nosotras	_____
vosotros/vosotras	_____
ustedes	_____
ellos/ellas	_____

Activity B

Fill in the blanks with the correct conjugated verb.

1   Marco y Ana _____ inglés.
    <u>hablar</u>

2   Nosotros _____ la Sagrada Familia.
    <u>visitar</u>

3   Yo _____ francés.
    <u>estudiar</u>

4   Catalina _____ el hotel.
    <u>pagar</u>

5   Usted _____ un buen restaurante.
    <u>buscar</u>

Activity C

Match the pronoun on the left with its verb on the right.

1	yo	a	hablamos
2	tú	b	visitáis
3	nosotros/nosotras	c	pago
4	vosotros/vosotras	d	estudian
5	ellos/ellas	e	buscas

> **SMART TIP**
>
> Have you noticed that each verb form is different in Spanish? Since the subject of the sentence can be inferred from the verb form, it is common to drop the pronoun. Instead of saying *Yo visito a mis amigos* (I visit my friends), you can simply say *Visito a mis amigos*.

Activity A
Label the following images.

1

_____

2

_____

3

_____

4

_____

Activity B
Rewrite each sentence in the negative.

1 Usted estudia español.

_____

2 La plancha funciona.

_____

3 Nosotros visitamos el Palacio Real.

_____

4 Las habitaciones son pequeñas.

_____

Activity C
Translate the phrases into Spanish.

1 my telephone _____

2 his room _____

3 their blankets _____

4 your (sing.) key _____

Activity D
Find the following words related to hotels in the word search.

ascensor	escritorio	llave
cama	habitación	manta
cómodo	hotel	planta
ducha	jabón	tele

```
J B W L L A V E F R W O A E I
S I T U B H A J A Q E B E Z W
B G S E P L S X A D B G O H B
M M E G L E C L R B E W R W M
E S K S P E E N V P O O O H A
S D W R B T N C O A B N O A N
C U V V O G S D W S R G S B T
R Y L H Q G O I U F M P U I A
I F V Q E M R M K C H E O T Z
T W Z B O S J O M Y H U W A P
O G W C F C C W U Z B A M C W
R Z V Q N A D L G B T Q C I D
I L C A E M B Y Q H W C V O P
O H X J D A P A A P G M V N C
R J G K P L A N T A I H M J J
```

Challenge
Now that you know how to conjugate –ar verbs, can you conjugate the following verbs: *preguntar*, *bailar*, *trabajar* and *amar*?

Internet Activity
Go online to **www.berlitzbooks.com/5Mtravel** to find a list of some of Spain's hotel chains. Browse through their websites and see if you can understand what kinds of rooms and services they offer.

Unit 5   Around Town

In this unit you will learn how to:
- talk about different places to visit.
- conjugate the verbs *ver* (to see) and *poder* (to be able to).
- get and follow directions.
- ask many different kinds of questions.

LESSON 1

En la ciudad

Dialogue

Listen to the following dialogue of a couple deciding on what to do during their stay in Madrid.

Ana	¿Qué vamos a hacer hoy?
Felipe	Yo tengo que ir al banco.
Ana	¿Podemos visitar el Palacio Real?
Felipe	¡Sí! Yo quisiera visitar una iglesia también!
Ana	¡Tenemos muchas cosas para hacer!

SMART TIP

If you're in a jam and can't think of the right word, try using *la cosa*, or "thing." For example, *¿Esta cosa qué es?* "What is this thing?" A few other ways of saying "thing" in Spanish are *el asunto* and *la cuestión*.

Activity A

Circle **T** for true and **F** for false.

1 Felipe y Ana están de vacaciones. **T**/ F
2 Ellos van a visitar un museo. T /**F**
3 Ellos van a visitar el Museo del Prado. T /**F**
4 Ellos tienen muchas cosas para hacer. **T**/ F

Activity B

Listen to the dialogue again and fill in the missing words.

¿Qué _____ a hacer hoy?

Yo tengo que ir _____.

¿Podemos _____ el Palacio Real?

¡Sí! Yo quisiera visitar _____ también.

¡Tenemos muchas _____ para hacer!

LESSON 2
Words to Know

Core Words

el banco	bank
el castillo	castle
el correo	post office
la iglesia	church
el mercado	market
el monumento	monument
el municipio	town hall [council]
el museo	museum
las oficinas de turismo	tourism office
el parque	park
el puente	bridge

Activity A
Label the following buildings.

1 _____

2 _____

3 _____

4 _____

Activity B
Where can you find the following?

1 maps of the city, information on tours, brochures

_____

2 fresh flowers, food, wine and cheese

_____

3 grass, trees, paths for walking

_____

4 paintings, sculptures, gift shops

_____

Activity C
Match the Spanish words with their English equivalents.

1	el museo	**a**	post office
2	el puente	**b**	town hall
3	el correo	**c**	bridge
4	el municipio	**d**	museum
5	el parque	**e**	market
6	el mercado	**f**	park

Your Turn
Use your new vocabulary to make a list of places you want to visit.

PARA VER
TO SEE

1. _____
2. _____
3. _____
4. _____

Smart Phrases

Core Phrases

¿En dónde está …?	Where is …?
el cajero automático más cercano	the nearest ATM
el banco	the bank
la oficina de cambio de divisas	the currency exchange office
Yo quisiera cambiar …por euros.	I want to exchange …for euros.
dólares	dollars
libras esterlinas	pounds
cheques de viajero	traveler's checks
¿Cuál es la tasa de cambio?	What is the exchange rate?
El cajero automático se comió mi tarjeta.	The ATM ate my card.
¿A qué hora abre/cierra el banco?	What time does the bank open/close?

Activity A

Fill in the blanks with the correct currency in Spanish.

1 Yo quisiera cambiar _____ por
   $
   _____.
   €

2 Yo quisiera cambiar _____ por
   £
   _____.
   $

3 Yo quisiera cambiar _____ por
   €
   _____.
   £

Activity B

Listen to the questions and write the number next to the correct answer.

____ El banco abre a las 9:00.

____ La tasa de cambio es 1 euro por un dólar cuarenta.

____ Hay un cajero automático en el banco.

____ El banco cierra a las 4:30.

Activity C

What do you say if…

1 …the ATM ate your card?

   _____

2 …you want to know when the bank opens?

   _____

3 …you want to exchange travelers checks for euros?

   _____

4 …you want to know where the nearest ATM is?

   _____

5 …you want to know the exchange rate?

   _____

6 …you want to know what time the bank closes?

   _____

Your Turn

Now that you can talk about exchanging money in Spanish, practice saying that you need to exchange money from your country's currency for euros.

Smart Grammar

The verbs *ver* and *poder*

The verb *ver* (to see) is irregular. The chart shows its conjugation in the present tense.

	ver	to see
yo	veo	I see
tú	ves	you see
usted	ve	you see
él/ella	ve	he/she sees
nosotros/nosotras	vemos	we see
vosotros/vosotras	veis	you see
ustedes	ven	you see
ellos/ellas	ven	they see

The verb *poder* (to be able to) is irregular. The chart shows its conjugation in the present tense.

	poder	to be able to
yo	puedo	I can
tú	puedes	you can
usted	puede	you can
él/ella	puede	he/she can
nosotros/nosotras	podemos	we can
vosotros/vosotras	podéis	you can
ustedes	pueden	you can
ellos/ellas	pueden	they can

SMART TIP

The verb *poder* can be followed by an infinitive if you want to say "to be able to do something." For example, *Nosotros podemos visitar el museo* means "We are able to (we can) visit the museum."

Activity A

Write a sentence in Spanish telling what the following people see.

1 (yo, el castillo) _____

2 (Juan, el mercado) _____

3 (nosotros, el puente) _____

4 (usted, el parque) _____

Activity B

Ana and Felipe have just arrived at the top of the Catedral de la Almudena. Help them use the verbs *ver* and *poder* to complete their dialogue.

Ana Yo _____ (ver) la Plaza de la Armería!

Felipe ¿En dónde? Yo no _____ (poder) verla.

Ana ¿Tú _____ (ver) el Palacio Real?

Felipe ¡Sí! ¡Nosotros _____ (ver) varios edificios!

Activity C

Answer the following questions in the affirmative.

1 ¿Pueden ustedes ir de vacaciones?

_____

2 ¿Véis vosotros el museo?

_____

3 ¿Podemos nosotros visitar el castillo?

_____

4 ¿Ven ustedes el cajero automático?

_____

5 ¿Puede la oficina de cambio de divisas cambiar dólares a euros?

_____

6 ¿Ven ellos el municipio?

_____

Las instrucciones

Dialogue

Listen to the following dialogue to learn how to ask for and understand directions.

Hombre Perdone, yo busco el Museo del Prado.

Mujer Yo le puedo ayudar. Tome la segunda calle a la derecha, continúe recto, y el museo está a su izquierda.

Hombre ¡Muchas gracias!

Mujer De nada.

SMART TIP

Here are some words you may need to get directions:

a la izquierda	to the left	*continúe*	continue
a la derecha	to the right	*atraviese*	cross
recto	straight ahead`	*sobre/en*	on
tome	take	*hacia*	toward
voltee	turn		

SMART TIP

De nada, literally "For nothing," is a polite way of saying "you're welcome" in Spanish.

Activity A

How would someone tell you to…

1 …turn left?

_____

2 …continue straight ahead?

_____

3 …turn right?

_____

4 …take your second left?

_____

Activity B

Look at the map below and follow the directions. Where is the final destination?

1 Comience (start) en el Museo del Prado. En la rotonda a la derecha, tome el Paseo del Prado hacia el norte. En la segunda rotonda, atraviese la calle de Alcalá y tome el Paseo de los Recoletos. Continúe recto cinco cuadras. El palacio está a su derecha.

Estoy en el _____.

2 Comience en la Puerta del Sol. Tome la calle de Alcalá hacia el este. Tome la sexta calle hacia la derecha en el Paseo del Prado. Continúe recto dos cuadras y el museo está a su derecha.

Estoy en el _____.

LESSON 6

Words to Know

El euro (The euro)

el billete	bill
el cambio	change
el centavo	cent
el dinero en efectivo	cash
la moneda	coin

Los números (Numbers)

You already know how to count from 1–60. Now you will learn from 70 on.

setenta	70
setenta y uno	71
setenta y dos	72
setenta y tres	73
setenta y cuatro	74
setenta y cinco	75
setenta y seis	76
setenta y siete	77
setenta y ocho	78
setenta y nueve	79
ochenta	80
ochenta y uno	81
ochenta y dos	82
noventa	90
noventa y uno	91
noventa y dos	92
cien	100
mil	1,000

SMART TIP

The numbers 70–99 are formed by naming the tens, for example, 70 is *setenta*, 80 is *ochenta*, and 90 is *noventa*, followed by the conjunction *y* (and) and the number for the unit, *uno, dos, tres,* etc. For example, 72 is *setenta y dos*, literally 70 and 2.

Activity A

Write how much money there is in each picture.

1 _____

2 _____

3 _____

4 _____

SMART TIPS

- Traditionally, the period and commas are inverted in Spanish prices. For example, $1,000.00 in English would be *$1.000,00* in Spanish. Often, the Spanish omit the thousands marker and just write *$1000,00*.

- To ask how much something costs in Spanish, say *¿Cuánto cuesta?*

Activity B

Write out the following prices in words.

1 €1.500,60 _____

2 €99,99 _____

3 €0,75 _____

Smart Phrases

- If you don't understand a certain word, say *¿Qué quiere decir…?* and say the word you don't understand. For example, if you want to know what *el puente* means, say *¿Qué quiere decir "el puente"?*
- If you bump into someone and want to apologize, say *perdone* or *disculpe*.

Core Phrases

Estoy perdido/perdida.	I am lost. (m/f)
Perdone, yo busco…	Excuse me, I am looking for…
¿Puede usted…?	Can you…?
hablar más lentamente	speak more slowly
repetirlo	repeat it
deletrearlo	spell it
escribirlo	write it
mostrarme en el mapa	show me on the map
indicarme el camino	give me directions
Lo siento, no entiendo.	I'm sorry, I don't understand.
¿Qué quiere decir eso?	What does that mean?

Activity A

Match the audio with what each person is saying.

a — I'm lost.

b — Can you speak more slowly? #__

#__

c — I'm looking for the Calle de Alcalá.

d — Can you spell it? #__

#__

Activity B

What do you say if…

1 …you want someone to repeat what they said?
_____

2 …you don't understand the word *el municipio*?
_____

3 …you are lost?
_____

4 …you don't understand?
_____

5 …you want someone to show you on the map?
_____

6 …you are looking for the bank?
_____

7 …you want someone to speak more slowly?
_____

8 …you want someone to give you directions?
_____

Your Turn

Imagine that you're having a difficult time understanding someone in Spanish. What can you say to the person so that he or she can help you understand better?

Smart Grammar

Question Words

The following words will help you ask questions in Spanish.

cómo	how
cuándo	when
cuánto	how much
cuántos/cuántas	how many (m/f pl.)
en dónde	where
porqué	why
qué	what
quién/quiénes	who (sing./pl.)

> **SMART TIP**
>
> A polite way of saying "What?" in Spanish is ¿Cómo? For example, if you don't understand something, you can say ¿Cómo? and the person will repeat himself.

Activity A

Write the question word associated with each image.

1

_____

2

_____

3

_____

4

_____

Activity B

Complete the questions with the correct question word.

1 ¿_____ cuesta?

2 ¿_____ se llama usted?

3 ¿_____ está el banco?

4 ¿_____ está en el coche con Federico?

Activity C

Match the English question words with their Spanish equivalents.

1	what		a	cómo
2	how much		b	en dónde
3	when		c	por qué
4	where		d	cuánto
5	why		e	qué
6	how		f	cuándo

Activity D

Complete the crossword puzzle with the Spanish equivalents of the words provided.

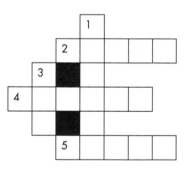

Across
2 who
4 how much
5 where

Down
1 when
3 what

Activity A
Label these different *monumentos*.

1

2

_____ _____

3

4

_____ _____

Activity B
Fill in the blanks with the correct form of the verb *poder*.

1 Nosotros _____ visitar la iglesia.

2 Vosotros _____ ir de vacaciones.

3 Yo _____ pagar en efectivo?

4 Ellas _____ ver el municipio.

Activity C
Complete the conjugation table for the verb *ver*.

yo	
	ves
usted	
él/ella	
	vemos
vosotros/vosotras	
	ven
ellos/ellas	

Activity D
What do you say if…

1 …you want someone to speak more slowly?

_____

2 …you want someone to write something down?

_____

3 …you want to know how much something costs?

_____

4 …you want to know where the church is?

_____

Activity E
Match the Spanish words with their English equivalents.

1	dónde	**a**	to see
2	ver	**b**	when
3	el mercado	**c**	to the right
4	cuando	**d**	where
5	el banco	**e**	to be able to
6	poder	**f**	bank
7	a la derecha	**g**	market

Challenge
Can you read the following numbers out loud without stopping?

1 692

2 1399

3 2010

4 77

Internet Activity
Go online to **www.berlitzbooks.com/5Mtravel** where you will find a link to online maps of Spain. Put in the address of a hotel in Madrid and then the address of a museum. See if you can understand the directions. If you want to get walking directions, make sure you choose *a pie*, "by foot."

In this unit you will learn:

- how to find a good restaurant.
- different food and drink.
- how to order in a café or restaurant.
- the verbs *pedir* (to ask for), *querer* (to want) and *beber* (to drink).

LESSON
1

¡A comer!

Dialogue

Listen to the following dialogue between Edward and the concierge.

Edward ¿Me puede aconsejar un restaurante?

Concierge ¿Desea usted algo en particular?

Edward Me encanta la comida española y francesa.

Concierge Hay una buena tapería al lado del correo.

Edward ¿Dónde está el correo? ¿Está lejos?

Concierge No señor, está frente a la iglesia.

CULTURE TIP

A *tapería* is a typical Spanish restaurant that serves a variety of foods in small portions that are eaten between main meals. The setting is relaxed and the prices are reasonable.

SMART TIP

Here are some more words to help with directions:

al lado de	next to
frente a	in front of
detrás	behind
lejos de	far from

Activity A
Complete the following sentences based on the dialogue.

1 Edward busca _____.

2 A él le encanta la comida _____ y _____.

3 Hay una buena _____ al lado del correo.

4 El correo está _____ la iglesia.

Activity B
Answer the questions in Spanish.

1 ¿Le gusta a Edward la comida italiana?

_____

2 ¿Hay una tapería al lado del correo?

_____

3 ¿Está la tapería lejos del correo?

_____

4 ¿Dónde está el correo?

_____

Activity C
Match the prepositions with their English equivalents.

1	lejos de	a	close to
2	detrás	b	behind
3	al lado de	c	far from
4	frente a	d	in front of
5	cerca de	e	next to
6	delante de	f	across from

Words to Know

Core Words

el desayuno	breakfast
el almuerzo	lunch
la cena	dinner
la comida	meal

Las entradas / Appetizers

la ensalada	salad
el pan	bread
la sopa	soup

Los pescados / Fish

el camarón	shrimp
el mejillón	mussel
el salmón	salmon
la vieira	scallop

Las carnes / Meat

el cerdo	pork
el cordero	lamb
el filete	steak
el pato	duck
el pollo	chicken
la carne de res	beef
la ternera	veal

Los postres / Desserts

el flan	caramel custard
la fruta	fruit
la tarta	pie
la torta	cake

Activity A

Label the food on the table below.

1
3
2
4
5

Activity B

Fill in the table with food you like and don't like.

Me gusta	No me gusta

SMART TIP

Don't get confused. In Spanish, *entrada* means "appetizer" and not "entree" as in "main dish." The main dish is called the *plato principal*.

CULTURE TIP

Note that in some Latin American countries another term for cake is *pastel*. "Birthday cake" is *pastel de cumpleaños*.

Smart Phrases

Core Phrases

Yo voy a pedir el/la _____.	I'll have the _____.
¿Me puede traer…, por favor?	May I please have…?
la cuenta	the check
un cuchillo	a knife
una cuchara	a spoon
un tenedor	a fork
una servilleta	a napkin
un vaso	a glass
¿Nos puede traer agua?	Can you bring us some water?
¿Tiene una carta en inglés?	Do you have an English menu?
Yo soy…	I am…
alérgico/alérgica a…	allergic to… (m/f)
vegetariano/vegetariana	vegetarian (m/f)
vegetariano puro/ vegetariana pura	vegan (m/f)
¿Dónde están los baños?	Where are the bathrooms?

Activity A

Label the following items in Spanish.

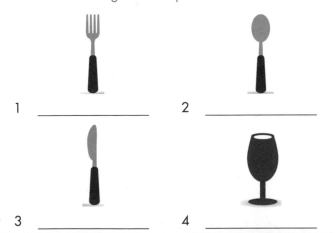

1 _____

2 _____

3 _____

4 _____

Activity B

What's missing from this table setting? Ask the waiter for what you need!

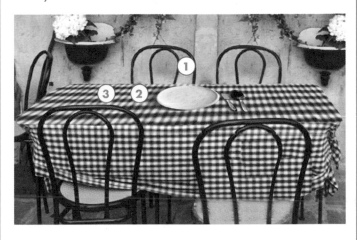

1 _____

2 _____

3 _____

Activity C

How do you…

1 …say you're a vegetarian?

_____

2 …ask for the check?

_____

3 …say you're allergic to shrimp?

_____

4 …order the salad?

_____

Your Turn

Now that you know how to order in a restaurant, use the vocabulary you've learned to practice ordering your favorite meal out loud. Don't forget to order something to drink, too!

LESSON 4
Smart Grammar

The verb *pedir* (to order/to ask for)

The verb *pedir* is regular. The chart shows its conjugation in the present tense.

	pedir	to order/to ask for
yo	pido	I order/ask for
tú	pides	you order/ask for
usted	pide	you order/ask for
él/ella	pide	he/she orders/asks for
nosotros/nosotras	pedimos	we order/ask for
vosotros/vosotras	pedís	you order/ask for
ustedes	piden	you order/ask for
ellos/ellas	piden	they order/ask for

Activity A

Fill in the blanks with the correct form of *ir + a pedir*.

1 ¿Qué _____ ellas?

2 Tú _____ la paella.

3 Yo _____ el pollo.

4 Nosotros _____ la cuenta.

5 Ellos _____ un taxi para ir al museo.

SMART TIPS

- When you're in a restaurant discussing what people are going to order, use the conjugated form of *ir + a pedir*. For example, *Yo voy a pedir…* "I'm going to order the…" *Juan va a pedir camarones al ajillo.* "Juan is going to order the shrimp with garlic sauce."

- When you're ordering, tell the waiter *Quiero…*, "I want…" It is also common to say *Tráigame una ensalada*, "Bring me a salad."

Activity B

Say what each person is ordering. Don't forget to use the correct form of *ir + a pedir*!

1

Juan _____.

2

Nosotros _____.

3

Vosotros _____.

Activity C

Answer the following questions in Spanish.

1 ¿Puede un vegetariano pedir carne o ensalada?
_____

2 Para comer la ensalada, ¿pides una cuchara o un tenedor?
_____

3 En España ¿qué pedimos primero, la entrada o el plato principal?
_____

4 ¿Pedimos desayuno por la noche?
_____

SMART TIP

If you want to use the word "or" in Spanish, say *o*. For example, *¿Quiere usted pato o pollo?* "Are you having duck or chicken?" Note that if the word that goes after the *o* begins with the letter "o," you use *u*. For example, *¿Quiere usted camarones u ostras?* "Are you having shrimp or oysters?"

56   Unit 6   Food and Drink

LESSON 5

En el restaurante

Dialogue

Cristina and Martín are trying to decide what to eat *en el restaurante* (at the restaurant). Listen to their conversation.

Cristina ¿Qué vas a pedir?

Martín Yo voy a pedir un filete. ¿Y tú?

Cristina Yo voy a pedir el almuerzo.

Martín ¿Qué vas a pedir de almuerzo?

Cristina Como entrada la ensalada y como plato principal el pollo.

Martín ¿Hay algún postre con el almuerzo?

Cristina Sí, yo voy a pedir el flan.

Martín ¿Quieres pedir una botella de vino?

Cristina ¡Encantada!

CULTURE TIP

The word *almuerzo* in a restaurant usually refers to a *prix-fixe* menu, where the appetizer, main dish and dessert are included in the price. Many restaurants in Spain and Latin America have *almuerzos*. The word *almuerzo*, however, can also simply mean "lunch."

SMART TIP

How do you like your steak? If you like it rare, say *rojo*; if you like it medium rare, say *tres cuartos*; if you like it medium, say *término medio*; if you like it well-done, say *bien cocido*.

Activity A

Match Cristina and Martín with the food they're going to order.

a

b

c

d

e

Activity B

What would you say if you want to order…

1 …a prix-fixe menu?

_____

2 …caramel custard for dessert?

_____

3 …the steak (well-done)?

_____

4 …a bottle of wine?

_____

Words to Know

Core Words

Las bebidas (Drinks)

el agua	water
el café	coffee
la cerveza	beer
el chocolate caliente	hot chocolate
la cola/cola de dieta	cola/diet cola
el jugo de naranja	orange juice
la leche	milk
el té	tea
el té helado	iced tea
el vino blanco/rojo	white/red wine

CULTURE TIP

If you order a *café* in Spanish, you'll get an espresso. If you want a less-concentrated American-style coffee, ask for a *café americano*. Note that *café americano* is usually served for breakfast.

Activity A

¿Qué piden ellos? Complete the sentences with the correct form of *pedir* and the name of the drink.

1 Jean _____.

2 Kathy y Michelle _____.

3 Nosotros _____.

4 Yo _____.

Activity B

Complete the crossword puzzle with the Spanish equivalents of the words provided.

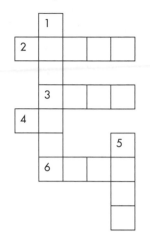

Across	**Down**
2 milk	1 beer
3 wine	5 coffee
4 tea	
6 water	

Activity C

Write what you like to drink with each meal.

el desayuno

_____

el almuerzo

_____

la cena

_____

Activity D

Match the Spanish words with their English equivalents.

1	el té	a	milk
2	la cerveza	b	tea
3	le leche	c	coffee
4	el agua	d	cola
5	la cola	e	water
6	el café	f	beer

Smart Phrases

Core Phrases

¿Qué le puedo servir?	What can I serve you?
Dígame.	What would you like? (lit. Tell me.)
¿Le gustaría…?	Would you like…?
un aperitivo	a cocktail/before-dinner drink
un digestivo	a liqueur/after-dinner drink
agua mineral	sparkling water
agua	still water
¡Buen provecho!	Enjoy your meal!
¿Ha terminado?	Are you finished?
¿Ha estado bien todo?	Was everything OK?

SMART TIP

Both *¿Ha terminado?* and *¿Ha estado bien todo?* use the past tense, which you will learn in Unit 10. To answer these questions, you can say *Sí, ya terminé*, "Yes, I'm finished," and *Sí, todo ha estado bien*, "Yes, everything was OK."

CULTURE TIP

While the tip is included in all restaurants/cafés in Spain and some Latin American countries, it is customary to leave some extra change (no more than 1 or 2 euros or a few coins in the local currency) for the *propina*, or "tip," if you are happy with the service.

Activity A

Put these questions/phrases you might hear from a waiter in the correct order.

_____ ¡Buen provecho!

_____ ¿Ha terminado?

_____ ¿Qué le puedo servir?

_____ ¿Estuvo bien todo?

Activity B

Fill in the blanks with the correct Spanish word.

1 ¿Le gustaría _____ (still water)?

2 ¿Le gustaría _____ (a cocktail)?

3 ¿Le gustaría _____ (sparkling water)?

4 ¿Le gustaría _____ (a liqueur)?

Activity C

Make up answers to the following questions and say them out loud.

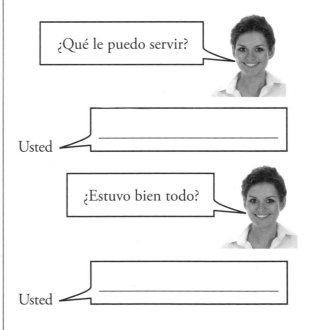

¿Qué le puedo servir?

Usted _____

¿Estuvo bien todo?

Usted _____

Smart Grammar

The verbs *querer* (to want) and *beber* (to drink)

The verb *querer* is irregular. The chart shows its conjugation in the present tense.

	querer	**to want**
yo	quiero	I want
tú	quieres	you want
usted	quiere	you want
él/ella	quiere	he/she wants
nosotros/nosotras	queremos	we want
vosotros/vosotras	queréis	you want
ustedes	quieren	you want
ellos/ellas	quieren	they want

The verb *beber* is regular. The chart shows its conjugation in the present tense.

	beber	**to drink**
yo	bebo	I drink
tú	bebes	you drink
usted	bebe	you drink
él/ella	bebe	he/she drinks
nosotros/nosotras	bebemos	we drink
vosotros/vosotras	bebéis	you drink
ustedes	beben	you drink
ellos/ellas	beben	they drink

SMART TIPS

- The conjugated verb *querer* is often followed by an infinitive to mean "to want to do something." For example, *¿Qué quieren comer ustedes?* "What do you want to eat?"

- If you want your salad without *aderezo* (dressing), or some dessert after your coffee, you'll need to learn some new prepositions. Here are some useful prepositions:

antes	before
después	after
con	with
sin	without

Activity A

Complete the conjugation table for the verb *querer*.

yo	
tú	
usted	
él/ella	
nosotros/nosotras	
vosotros/vosotras	
ustedes	
ellos/ellas	

Activity B

Complete the conjugation table for the verb *beber*.

yo	
tú	
usted	
él/ella	
nosotros/nosotras	
vosotros/vosotras	
ustedes	
ellos/ellas	

Activity C

Fill in the blanks with the correct form of *querer*.

1 Hernán _____ ir de vacaciones.

2 Yo _____ agua mineral.

3 José Miguel y Juan _____ chocolate caliente.

4 Nosotros _____ ir al museo.

Activity D

Fill in the blanks with the correct form of *beber*.

1 Meghan _____ vino blanco con la cena.

2 Vosotros _____ agua.

3 Tú _____ un café después de la comida.

4 Ellas _____ un aperitivo antes de la comida.

Unit 6 Review

Activity A

How do you...

1 ...ask for the check?

_____

2 ...order the chicken?

_____

3 ...say that you drink coffee?

_____

4 ...ask where the bathroom is?

_____

Activity B

Label the following food and drink.

1

_____

2

_____

3

_____

4

_____

Activity C

Choose the word that doesn't belong in each group.

1 la tarta
   el cuchillo
   el flan
2 el mejillón
   el café
   el chocolate caliente
3 un tenedor
   una cuchara
   un digestivo

Activity D

Write the Spanish translation of each word, and then arrange the circled letters to find a bonus word.

1 chocolate: __ __ __ __ __ __ __ ◯ __

2 coffee: __ ◯ __ __

3 spoon: __ __ __ __ __ ◯ __ __

4 fork: ◯ __ __ __ __ __ __

5 bread: __ ◯ __ __

Bonus word: __ __ __ __ __

Activity E

Fill in the blanks with the correct form of the verb given.

1 Abdellah _____ (querer) beber agua.

2 Nosotros _____ (beber) jugo de naranja.

3 Vosotros _____ (pedir) el pescado.

4 Ellos _____ (querer) ir a un restaurante.

5 Yo _____ (beber) café después de la cena.

6 Tú _____ (pedir) un té helado.

> **Challenge**
>
> Can you conjugate the verbs *pedir*, *querer* and *beber* without checking in the book?

Internet Activity

Go online to **www.berlitzbooks.com/5Mtravel** where you will find the links to menus from some of the most famous restaurants in Barcelona. Start planning your dinner ahead of time!

Unit 7 Shopping & Souvenirs

In this unit you will learn:
- how to shop in Spanish-speaking countries.
- ideas for souvenirs.
- new adjectives and how to use them.
- how to conjugate *–er* and *–ar* verbs.

LESSON 1
¡Vayamos de compras!

The Souvenir Shop

Emma is in a souvenir shop looking for presents for her friends.

> **SMART TIP**
> The word *souvenir* is a French word often used in Spanish. The word *recuerdo* is actually the Spanish word, which means "a memory."

Sombrero cordobés 15€
Muñeca bailaora de flamenco 8€
Globo de nieve torero 10€
Camiseta Madrid 8€
MADRID
MADRID

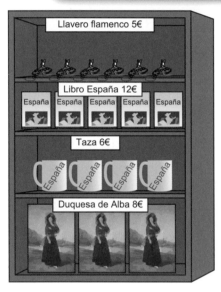

Llavero flamenco 5€
Libro España 12€
España España España España España
Taza 6€
España España España España
Duquesa de Alba 8€

Activity A
What can Emma buy for…?

1 Ricardo – *él ama el arte*
   _____

2 Sara – *ella ama la moda* (fashion)
   _____

3 Tomás – *él ama leer* (to read)
   _____

4 Mónica – *ella ama beber café*
   _____

Activity B
Emma only has 20€. Is that enough to buy…

1 la muñeca bailaora de flamenco y el sombrero cordobés?   **Sí/No**

2 La Duquesa de Alba y la taza?   **Sí/No**

3 la camiseta y el libro?   **Sí/No**

4 la muñeca flamenca y el llavero?   **Sí/No**

Activity C
Which souvenirs would you buy for your friends?

1 _____
2 _____
3 _____

Words to Know

Core Words

los almacenes/la tienda de departamentos	department store
la boutique	store [shop]
el centro comercial	shopping mall [centre]
la farmacia	pharmacy
la floristería	flower shop
la joyería	jewelry store [jeweller's]
la librería	bookstore
la licorería	wine store
la panadería	bakery
el supermercado	supermarket
la tabaquería	tobacco shop [smoke shop]
la tienda de abarrotes	grocery store
la tienda…	…store [shop]
de antigüedades	antique
de chocolates	chocolate/candy
de perfumes	perfume
de ropa	clothing
de souvenirs/ de recuerdos	souvenir

CULTURE TIPS

- Some of the most popular department stores in Spain include *Corte Inglés* and *Galerías Preciado* and some of the most popular supermarkets are *Mercado de San Miguel*, *¡Viva la Vida!* and *Capperi Gourmet*.
- There is much more than just cigarettes in a *tabaquería*. You can find phone cards, stamps and often bus or *metro* tickets.

Activity A
Label each of the stores below.

1 _____

2 _____

3 _____

4 _____

Activity B
Fill in the blanks with the correct store names.

1 Cecilia y Adriana buscan _____.
                    the shopping mall

2 Yo busco _____.
             the chocolate store

3 Usted busca _____.
             the bookstore

4 Nosotros buscamos _____.
            the perfume store

Activity C
Match each item with the store where you can buy it.

1	earrings	a	la licorería
2	flowers	b	la joyería
3	perfume	c	la farmacia
4	wine	d	la floristería
5	aspirin	e	la tienda de perfumes

Smart Phrases

Core Phrases

¿Puede mostrarme esto/eso?	Can you show me this/that?
¿Es verdadero?	Is it real?
Sólo estoy mirando.	I'm just browsing.
¿Cuánto cuesta eso?	How much does that cost?
¿Puedo pagar con tarjeta?	Can I pay with a credit card?
¿En dónde está la caja?	Where is the cashier?
Es demasiado caro.	It's too expensive.
¿Es su mejor precio?	Is that your best price?
Sólo tengo ____ euros.	I have only ____ euros.
¿Me puede dar un descuento?	Can you give me a discount?
Tengo que pensarlo.	I have to think about it.

SMART TIP

Want to ask to see <u>this</u> shirt or <u>that</u> piece of jewelry? Here are the words you'll need to know:

- este/ese (if the noun begins with a vowel) (m sing.)
- esta/esa (f sing.)
- estos/estas (m/f pl.)

Activity A

Match the phrases below with the person who is speaking.

1 _____

2 _____

3 _____

?

4 _____

a ¿Puedo pagar con tarjeta?

b ¿Cuánto cuesta eso?

c ¿Me puede mostrar eso?

d Es demasiado caro.

Activity B

What do you say if...

1 ...you want to try to get a discount?

_____

2 ...you need to think about it?

_____

3 ...you're just browsing?

_____

4 ...you have only 20€?

_____

Smart Grammar

Regular –er and –ar verbs in the present tense

To conjugate –er verbs, remove the –er ending and add the following endings.

	escoger	**to choose**
yo	escoj**o**	I choose
tú	escog**es**	you choose
usted	escog**e**	you choose
él/ella	escog**e**	he/she chooses
nosotros/nosotras	escog**emos**	we choose
vosotros/vosotras	escog**éis**	you choose
ustedes	escog**en**	you choose
ellos/ellas	escog**en**	they choose

To conjugate –ar verbs, remove the –ar ending and add the following endings.

	comprar	**to buy**
yo	compr**o**	I buy
tú	compr**as**	you buy
usted	compr**a**	you buy
él/ella	compr**a**	he/she buys
nosotros/nosotras	compr**amos**	we buy
vosotros/vosotras	compr**áis**	you buy
ustedes	compr**an**	you buy
ellos/ellas	compr**an**	they buy

Here are some regular –er and –ar verbs:

castigar	to punish
engordar	to gain weight
esperar	to wait (for)
perder	to lose
recoger	to pick up/gather
responder	to answer
terminar	to finish
vender	to sell

Activity A

Conjugate the verb *vender*.

yo   _____

tú   _____

usted   _____

él/ella   _____

nosotros(as)   _____

vosotros(as)   _____

ustedes   _____

ellos/ellas   _____

Activity B

Conjugate the verb *terminar*.

yo   _____

tú   _____

usted   _____

él/ella   _____

nosotros(as)   _____

vosotros(as)   _____

ustedes   _____

ellos/ellas   _____

Activity C

Fill in the blanks with the correct conjugated verb.

1 Frank _____ (*esperar*) a Elena en la joyería.

2 Nosotros _____ (*responder*) respondemos el teléfono.

3 Vosotros _____ (*terminar*) vuestra comida.

4 Ellos _____ (*engordar*) en los restaurantes de España.

> **SMART TIP**
>
> In Spanish, the g, as in *escoger*, changes to "*j*" when it precedes an a, o, or u. So, "I choose" is *yo escojo*.

LESSON 5
La ropa

DAMAS

CABALLEROS

El abrigo 45€

El jean 50€

La chaqueta 75€

La corbata 20€

El bolso 60€

El pantalón 39€

El cinturón 20€

La camisa 30€

Fashion

Esteban needs to buy presents for his friends and they all want the latest fashion from Madrid.

Activity A

Esteban only has 100€ to spend. Which combination of gifts can he buy?

a el cinturón, el bolso, la corbata

b el abrigo, el pantalón, el jean

c la camisa, la chaqueta, el abrigo

Activity B

If you had 100€ to spend on gifts for yourself or others, what would you buy?

_____

_____

_____

Activity C

Write the total price of:

el bolso

el pantalón

la camisa

la chaqueta

_____ €

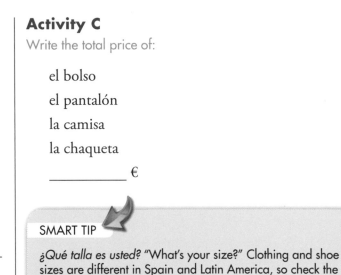

SMART TIP

¿Qué talla es usted? "What's your size?" Clothing and shoe sizes are different in Spain and Latin America, so check the glossary for conversion charts.

Activity D

Find all the words from the image above in the word search.

```
V F I Z K K F D R R M N P Q V B C W Y T Z G T C V S N T P A
U Q B T T N N F X V O P L I J N B H O T M D Q O U T L Q L F
W C Y D D G Y G U R T H V I K T M S A Q C Q B R L K T P L U
N V L A J A Y S U F X Z Q P R K I R B Q G G V D B Y H Y N Y Z
H Q J O C P N T O B H B G E J T U I C I U B S A P W H T O B
P C U C Z Z N G J H X M Z R G A Y J O C A E L T S U Q X R D
C F D W Y I W S W W G F O M W I T P P G P O T A O Y Y F T L
R O H I C U D W Q Z N I Y J T N Q P Q P N Y S A D S A U C O
M Q L E W Y L W D M Z Y A R G Y U D Q W K N T T R O V B A G
J P H N E T J P I S R K Q L J S Y H Z X R A J H O Z R B Q X
A S I M A C C H D P R U J Z P Z G H C U H E D O X N R V O V
I T Y N X J K L J O J E N E J X J Q D G R J X Y S I F B O E
K B C E S R V F X D O B T S S H G Y X F E F K C G L S H C F
S L S S S L Z E P G O X I M R E Y P L T X Y D O V L O F X A
M F Q U Q V B W I D H G N X E D I I P A N T A L O N N B J C
```

66 Unit 7 Shopping & Souvenirs

LESSON 6

Words to Know

Core Words

la botella (de vino)	bottle (of wine)
la caja de chocolates	box of chocolates
la camiseta	T-shirt
el dibujo	drawing
la joya	piece of jewelry
el juguete	toy
el libro	book
el llavero	keychain
la mascada	scarf
el perfume	perfume/cologne
la pintura	painting
los productos de belleza	beauty products
la ropa	clothing
el suéter	sweater
la tarjeta postal	postcard

Activity A

Complete the sentences with the correct souvenir.

1 Bernardo quiere comprar _____
   en la joyería.   *piece of jewelry*

2 Lorenzo quiere comprar un _____
   para Octavio.   *toy*

3 Josefina quiere comprar _____.
                beauty products

4 David quiere comprar una _____
   en la tienda de tabaco.   *post card*

Activity B

Listen to what each person is looking for and label the correct item.

#__   #__   #__

Activity C

Match the Spanish word to the English word.

1	el cuadro	a	drawing
2	el juguete	b	scarf
3	el dibujo	c	painting
4	la mascada	d	toy

Activity D

Make a list of the souvenirs you want to bring home for your friends and family.

RECUERDOS PARA COMPRAR

_____
_____
_____
_____
_____
_____
_____
_____

CULTURE TIP

IVA (*impuesto al valor agregado*) is the value-added tax that is included in all the prices you see in stores and restaurants. There is no additional tax—the price you see is the price you pay.

Smart Phrases

CULTURE TIP

Make sure you check out the souvenirs of the different regions in Spain, as well as of some Latin American countries. For example, try the wine in the region of *La Rioja* or the pottery in *Andalucía* in Spain, the wine and food in Argentina and Chile, the wool sweaters and handcrafts in Ecuador, the chocolate in Venezuela, etc.

Core Phrases

Yo quisiera algo de esta región.	I would like something from this region.
¿Le gusta?	Do you like it?
Sí, me gusta.	Yes, I like it.
¿Puede usted enviarlo/ envolverlo?	Can you ship/ wrap it?
¿Puede usted envolverlo para regalo?	Can you gift-wrap it?
Es un regalo.	It's a present.
Son ____ euros.	The total is ____ euros.
Voy a pagar en efectivo.	I'll pay in cash.
Aquí está su cambio.	Here is your change.

Activity B
How do you say…

1 …you want something from this region?
   a Yo lo quiero envuelto para regalo.
   b Yo quisiera alguna cosa de esta región.
2 …you will pay in cash?
   a Voy a pagar con una tarjeta.
   b Voy a pagar en efectivo.
3 …it's a present?
   a Es un regalo.
   b Si, me gusta.

Activity A
Match the saleswoman's responses with Manuel's questions.

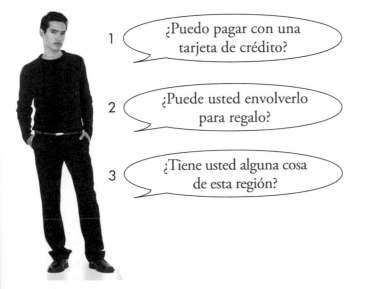

1 ¿Puedo pagar con una tarjeta de crédito?
2 ¿Puede usted envolverlo para regalo?
3 ¿Tiene usted alguna cosa de esta región?

a Sí, ¿es para regalar?
b Sí, nosotros tenemos productos de esta región.
c Hay que pagar en efectivo.

Smart Grammar

Adjectives

grande	big
pequeño/pequeña	small (m/f)
lindo/linda	beautiful (m/f)
bonito/bonita	pretty (m/f)
feo/fea	ugly (m/f)
nuevo/nueva	new (m/f)
simpático/simpática	nice (m/f)
bueno/buena	good (m/f)
malo/mala	bad (m/f)
caro/cara	expensive (m/f)
jóven	young
viejo/vieja	old (m/f)

Los colores (Colors)

blanco/blanca	white (m/f)
negro/negra	black (m/f)
gris	grey
rojo/roja	red (m/f)
anaranjado/anaranjada	orange (m/f)
amarillo/amarilla	yellow (m/f)
verde	green
azul	blue
morado/morada	purple (m/f)
rosado/rosada	pink (m/f)
marrón	brown

SMART TIPS

- In Spanish, adjectives usually go after nouns. However, they sometimes go before nouns, often when someone is trying to sound eloquent or poetic. For example, "the black night" can be *la negra noche*.
- Adjectives must always agree with the number and gender of the noun. For example, *dos libros pequeños* (two small books) or *dos mascadas negras* (two black masks). Note that *pequeños* and *negras* go after the noun.

Activity A

Complete the sentences with the correct adjective.

1 María busca un _____ cuadro.
   beautiful

2 Los perfumes son demasiado _____.
   expensive

3 La camiseta es demasiado _____.
   small

4 Esta mascada es _____.
   ugly

Activity B

Describe the articles of clothing below. Remember that the color goes after the noun.

1 _____   2 _____

3 _____   4 _____

Unit 7 Review

Activity A
Label the following stores.

1 _____   2 _____

3 _____   4 _____

Activity B
How do you ask...

1 ...how much something costs?

_____

2 ...if something is real?

_____

3 ...if you can get a discount?

_____

4 ...where the cash register is?

_____

Challenge

Can you conjugate the following –er and –ar verbs?

1 *comer* = to eat

2 *comprar* = to buy

3 *escuchar* = to hear

Activity C
Choose the correct translation for the underlined word.

1 Marco busca <u>un juguete</u>.
   a book   **b** toy

2 Abdellah busca <u>una corbata</u>.
   a shirt   **b** tie

3 Santiago busca <u>un llavero</u>.
   a keychain   **b** bottle of wine

4 Cecilia busca <u>un cuadro</u>.
   a painting   **b** drawing

Activity D
Draw a picture of:

1 un coche negro pequeño
2 una botella grande de vino
3 un lindo jean azul

Internet Activity

Go online to **www.berlitzbooks.com/5Mtravel** to look at some of the latest fashion magazines in Spanish editions. Print out a page and see if you can label all the articles of clothing!

Unit 8 Technology

In this unit you will learn how to:
- talk about different kinds of technology.
- conjugate the verbs *hacer* (to do, to make), *decir* (to say), *escribir* (to write) and *leer* (to read).
- use a computer and have a phone conversation.

LESSON 1
La tecnología

Dialogue

Robert has been in Colombia for a few days and wants to find an Internet café so that he can e-mail his family to tell them what a wonderful time he's having. Listen to his conversation with the hotel concierge.

Roberto	¿Hay un cibercafé cerca del hotel? Yo quiero leer mi correo electrónico.
Concierge	Sí señor, hay un cibercafé al frente.
Roberto	¿Tienen servicio de WiFi? Yo tengo mi ordenador portátil.
Concierge	Hay WiFi gratuito en el café al final de la calle.
Roberto	¡Perfecto! Muchas gracias.

CULTURE TIPS

- Many of the larger cities in Spain now have free WiFi zones in parks and near monuments. Look for signs that say *Zona Wi-Fi* and stay connected for free!

- If you are traveling in Latin America you will find that the term used for "computer" is *computadora*, and "laptop" is *computadora portátil*.

Activity A
Circle the correct answer.

1 Robert busca _____.
   a un cibercafé   **b un correo electrónico**

2 Hay un cibercafé _____.
   a a la izquierda   **b al frente**

3 Hay WiFi gratuito _____.
   a en un café   **b en el cibercafé**

Activity B
Listen to the dialogue again and fill in the missing words.

Roberto	¿Hay un _____ cerca del hotel? Yo quiero _____ mi correo electrónico.
Concierge	Sí. Hay un _____ al frente.
Roberto	¿Tienen servicio de WiFi ? Yo tengo mi _____.
Concierge	Hay _____ en el café al final de la calle.
Roberto	¡Perfecto! _____.

Activity C
Answer the following questions in Spanish.

1 Why is Robert looking for an Internet café?

_____

2 Is there an Internet café near the hotel?

_____

3 Why should Robert go to the café at the end of the street instead?

_____

LESSON 2
Words to Know

Core Words

el adaptador	adapter
el celular	cell phone [mobile]
el cibercafé	Internet café
el correo electrónico	e-mail
la impresora	printer
el Internet	Internet
la memoria de USB	USB key/flash drive
el ordenador/ la computadora	computer (SP/LA)
el ordenador portátil/la computadora portátil	laptop (SP/LA)
la pantalla	screen
el ratón	mouse
el teclado	keyboard
la tecnología	technology
el WiFi	WiFi

Extra Words

al frente	across the way
al final de	at the end of

Activity A
Circle the best response.

1 Where do you go to check your e-mail?

   a el cibercafé   **b el ratón**

2 What kind of computer can you carry around with you?

   a el celular   **b el ordenador portátil**

3 What do you use if your plug doesn't fit?

   a el adaptador   **b la pantalla**

Activity B
Can you solve these riddles? Write the correct answers in Spanish.

1 You can drag me around if you want to open a window.

   _____

2 I can write and draw but have no hands.

   _____

3 I can blink but have no eyes.

   _____

4 I have keys and locks but open no doors.

   _____

5 You can surf me but I have no waves.

   _____

Activity C
Label the following images.

1 _____   2 _____

3 _____   4 _____

SMART PRONUNCIATIONS

- The acronym *USB* is pronounced *oo–ese–beh*.
- *WiFi* is pronounced *wee-fee*, but *wai-fai* as in English is not uncommon.

Smart Phrases

Core Phrases

Yo necesito mandar un correo electrónico.	I need to send an e-mail.
Yo necesito descargar un documento.	I need to download a document.
¿Cuánto cuestan 30 minutos de acceso?	What is the price for 30 minutes of access?
¿Hay WiFi en este hotel?	Do you have WiFi at this hotel?
¿Hay puntos de WiFi gratuitos?	Are there free hotspots?
¿Puedo imprimir mi boleto de embarque?	Can I print my boarding pass?
¿Dónde puedo comprar un paquete prepago de Internet?	Where can I buy a prepaid Internet package?

CULTURE TIP

For WiFi access on your laptop, you can buy a prepaid package from cell phone and Internet providers. There are two main types of plans, by volume of information downloaded, and by time. The prices start at around 20€, more than what you would pay at a *cibercafé*, but a good option if you want Internet access 24/7.

SMART TIP

If you want to say you *only* have something, use the word *solamente* or *sólo*, or use the expression *no…más que*. For example, *Yo tengo solamente/sólo tres euros* or *Yo no tengo más que tres euros* means "I only have three euros."

Activity A

What do you say if you want to…

1 …know if there are free hotspots?

_____

2 …know how much 10 minutes of access costs?

_____

3 …send an e-mail?

_____

4 …know where to buy a prepaid Internet package?

_____

Activity B

Write the appropriate Spanish questions to complete the conversation.

1 _____ ?

2 _____ ?

3 _____ ?

4 _____ ?

Los treinta minutos cuestan 5€.

No tenemos WiFi en este hotel.

Sí, usted puede imprimir.

Tenemos puntos de WiFi gratuitos.

LESSON 4 — Smart Grammar

The verb *hacer* (to do, to make)

The verb *hacer* (to do, to make) is irregular. The chart shows its conjugation in the present tense.

yo	hago	I do/make
tú	haces	you do/make
usted	hace	you do/make
él/ella	hace	he/she does/makes
nosotros/nosotras	hacemos	we do/make
vosotros/vosotras	hacéis	you do/make
ustedes	hacen	you do/make
ellos/ellas	hacen	they do/make

While the verb *hacer* is normally translated as "to do" or "to make," it can have different meanings when used with expressions such as:

hacer deporte	to play/practice sports
hacer fila	to stand in line
hacer compras	to go shopping

Activity A

Fill in the blanks with the correct form of *hacer*.

1 Jacobo _____ sus maletas.

2 Tú _____ deporte.

3 Vosotros _____ las cuentas.

4 Hoy _____ un lindo día.

5 Yo _____ fila.

6 Ellas _____ un recorrido de la ciudad.

SMART TIP

¿*Cómo está el tiempo?* How's the weather?

Hacer is also used to talk about the weather in Spanish. For example, *Hace calor* means "It's hot" and *Hace frío* means "It's cold." Here are a few other examples:

Hace buen día.	It's nice out.
Hace mal tiempo.	The weather is bad.
Hace sol.	It's sunny out.

Activity B

Circle the letter of the correct phrase.

1
    a Él hace deporte.
    b Él hace compras.

2
    a Nosotros hacemos deporte.
    b Nosotros hacemos fila.

3
    a Ella hace compras.
    b Ella hace fila.

4
    a Yo hago mis maletas.
    b Yo hago un viaje.

Activity C

How do you say…

1 …the weather is nice?

_____

2 …it's cold out?

_____

3 …it's hot out?

_____

4 …the weather is bad?

_____

Bill has just bought a *tarjeta telefónica* and is making a phone call from a payphone. Follow along with the instructions he sees on the phone.

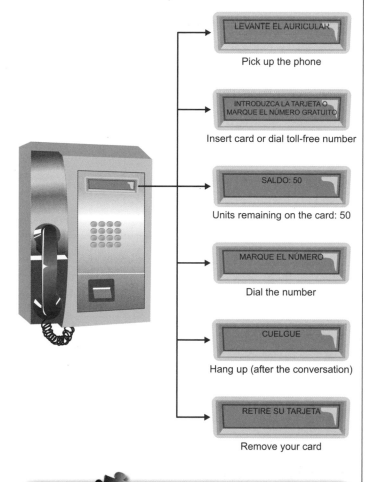

LEVANTE EL AURICULAR	Pick up the phone
INTRODUZCA LA TARJETA O MARQUE EL NÚMERO GRATUITO	Insert card or dial toll-free number
SALDO: 50	Units remaining on the card: 50
MARQUE EL NÚMERO	Dial the number
CUELGUE	Hang up (after the conversation)
RETIRE SU TARJETA	Remove your card

CULTURE TIP

If you're used to putting change in a pay phone to make a call, you'll notice that the phones in Spain are quite different. To make local calls, you'll need a calling card called *una tarjeta telefónica*. *Las tarjetas telefónicas* come with either 50 or 120 *unidades* ("units") and can be purchased at tobacco shops and post offices. If you plan on making international calls, a *tarjeta telefónica internacional* has much better international rates.

Activity A

Circle **T** for true or **F** for false.

1 Calling cards in Spain come in 20 and 30 units. **T / F**

2 Public phones in Spain do not take coins. **T / F**

3 A *tarjeta telefónica* is best for making international calls. **T / F**

4 A toll-free number is called a *número verde*. **T / F**

Activity B

Put the following steps in the correct order for making a phone call.

_____ Cuelgue

_____ Levante el auricular

_____ Marque el número

_____ Retire su tarjeta

_____ Introduzca la tarjeta o marque el número gratuito

Activity C

What do you do when the phone indicates:

1 **levante el auricular?**
   a Pick up the phone.
   b Hang up the phone.

2 **marque el número?**
   a Insert your card.
   b Dial the number.

3 **cuelgue?**
   a Pick up the phone.
   b Hang up the phone.

4 **retire su tarjeta?**
   a Insert your card.
   b Remove your card.

SMART TIP

To make a call from Spain to the US, dial 00 + 1 + area code + phone number. To call the UK, dial 00 + 44 + area code + phone number.

LESSON 6

Words to Know

Core Words

abrir	to open
apagar	to turn off
el archivo	file
borrar	to delete
conectar	to connect
la contraseña	password
descargar	to download
el enlace	link
enviar	to send
escribir	to type
guardar	to save
hacer click	to click
imprimir	to print
mensaje nuevo	new message
prender	to turn on
el programa	software
el sitio Web	website

Activity A

Write the verb associated with each image.

1

_____

2

_____

3

_____

4

_____

Activity B

Complete the crossword puzzle.

Across

4 software

Down

1 to connect

2 to send

3 link

Activity C

Circle the best response.

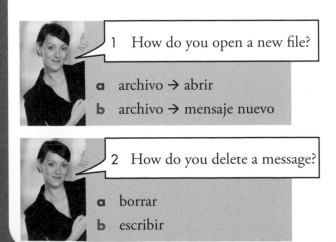

1 How do you open a new file?

  a archivo → abrir

  b archivo → mensaje nuevo

2 How do you delete a message?

  a borrar

  b escribir

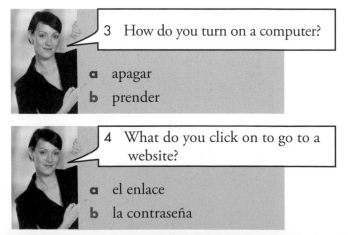

3 How do you turn on a computer?

  a apagar

  b prender

4 What do you click on to go to a website?

  a el enlace

  b la contraseña

Smart Phrases

Core Phrases

¿Aló?	Hello?
¿Quién habla?	Who's calling?
Es ____.	It's ____ calling.
Puedo hablar con ____?	May I speak with ____?
Un momento por favor.	Please hold.
Se lo/la paso.	I'll get him/her.
Él/ella no está aquí.	He/She is not here.
¿Quiere dejar un mensaje?	Would you like to leave a message?
Dígale que me llame, por favor.	Ask him/her to call me back, please.
Ha marcado el número equivocado.	You have the wrong number.

Activity A

Match the questions from column A with the correct responses in column B.

1 ¿Quiere dejar un mensaje?

2 ¿Puedo hablar con Julia?

3 ¿Quién llama?

a Ella no está aquí.

b Es Virginia.

c Dígale que me llame, por favor.

SMART TIP

Note that *aló* is only used to say hello when you answer the phone. To say "hello" in person, say *hola* at any time if you are friends, or *buenos días* during the day, *buenas tardes* in the afternoon, and *buenas noches* in the evening.

Activity B

Ramón is calling to speak with Ana. Help him by completing the conversation.

¿Aló? ¿Quién llama?

_____

Buenos días Ramón.

_____

Un momento, por favor. Se la paso.

Activity C

How do you…

1 …introduce yourself on the phone?

_____

2 …say "you have the wrong number"?

_____

3 …say hello when you pick up the phone?

_____

4 …ask for someone to call you back?

_____

Smart Grammar

The verbs *decir* (to say), *escribir* (to write) and *leer* (to read)

The verb *decir* (to say) is irregular. The chart shows its conjugation in the present tense.

	decir	to say
yo	digo	I say
tú	dices	you say
usted	dice	you say
él/ella	dice	he/she says
nosotros/nosotras	decimos	we say
vosotros/vosotras	decís	you say
ustedes	dicen	you say
ellos/ellas	dicen	they say

The verb *escribir* (to write) is regular. The chart shows its conjugation in the present tense.

	escribir	to write
yo	escribo	I write
tú	escribes	you write
usted	escribe	you write
él/ella	escribe	he/she writes
nosotros/nosotras	escribimos	we write
vosotros/vosotras	escribís	you write
ustedes	escriben	you write
ellos	escriben	they write

The verb *leer* (to read) is irregular. The chart shows its conjugation in the present tense.

	leer	to read
yo	leo	I read
tú	lees	you read
usted	lee	you read
él/ella	lee	he/she reads
nosotros/nosotras	leemos	we read
vosotros/vosotras	leéis	you read
ustedes	leen	you read
ellos/ellas	leen	they read

Activity A

Write the Spanish equivalent next to the English phrase.

I write _____

you read _____

she says _____

we write _____

you (pl.) read _____

they say _____

Activity B

Answer the following questions in Spanish.

1 ¿Escribes tú a tus amigos (friends)?

_____

2 ¿Lees tu correo con frecuencia (often)?

_____

3 ¿Qué dices cuando contestas el teléfono?

_____

Activity C

Describe in Spanish what each person is doing.

1  Martín _____.

2  Manuela _____.

3  ¡Buenos días! Vicente _____.

Unit 8   Review

Activity A
How do you ask...

1   ...if there is an Internet café near your hotel?

_____

2   ...where to buy a prepaid Internet package?

_____

3   ...if you can print your boarding pass?

_____

4   ...to speak with someone on the phone?

_____

Activity B
Complete the verb chart.

	escribir	leer
yo		
tú		
usted		
él/ella		
nosotros/nosotras		
vosotros/vosotras		
ustedes		
ellos/ellas		

Activity C
Match the Spanish word in the left column to its English equivalent in the right column.

1	borrar	**a**	to click
2	hacer click	**b**	to pick up the phone
3	levantar el auricular	**c**	to dial
4	prender	**d**	to delete
5	marcar el número	**e**	to turn on
6	colgar	**f**	to save
7	guardar	**g**	to hang up the phone

Activity D
Describe each picture in Spanish.

1

Ellos _____

2

Ella _____

3

Nosotros _____

4

Yo _____

> **Challenge**
> Can you make up your own phone conversation in Spanish? Pretend you're calling to talk to a friend and say the dialogue out loud.

Internet Activity
Want to learn how to write the accents in Spanish? Go to **www.berlitzbooks.com/5Mtravel** for a list of websites that will help you learn how to type Spanish accents or change your keyboard layout.

Unit 9 Nightlife

In this unit you will learn how to:
- talk about different nightlife options.
- use the prepositions *a* and *de*.
- strike up a conversation with a stranger.
- conjugate the verbs *decidir* (to decide) and *salir* (to go out).

LESSON 1

¡Salgamos!

Dialogue

Aldo and Natalia are trying to figure out how to spend their first evening on vacation. Listen to their conversation.

Aldo	¿Qué quieres hacer esta noche?
Natalia	¡Quiero salir!
Aldo	¿Adónde quieres ir?
Natalia	Yo quiero bailar. ¿Podemos ir a un club nocturno?
Aldo	Sí, pero yo no puedo quedarme hasta muy tarde.

> **SMART TIP**
>
> *Muy tarde* means "too/very late," but if you don't want to leave too early, use the word *muy pronto*. For example, *¡Yo no quiero salir muy pronto!* means "I don't want to go out too early!"

Activity A

Answer the following questions in Spanish.

1 ¿Qué quiere hacer Natalia esta noche?

_____

2 ¿Adónde quiere ir?

_____

Activity B

You are having a conversation with Aldo. Tell him what you want to do tonight.

¿Qué quieres hacer esta noche?

_____.
— Ustedes

¿Adónde quieres ir?

_____.
— Ustedes

¿Podemos ir a un club nocturno?

_____.
— Ustedes

> **CULTURE TIP**
>
> If you plan on staying out late, make sure you know how you're going to get home. Public transportation late at night in Spanish cities often runs on a limited schedule. You can always ask where the nearest taxi stand is.

LESSON 2
Words to Know

Core Words

el bar	bar
el café	café
el casino	casino
el cine	movie theater
el club de jazz	jazz club
el club nocturno	night club
el concierto	concert
el teatro	theater [theatre]

Activity A

Choose the correct answer.

1   If you want to play poker, you should go to:

    a el casino   **b** el cine

2   If you want to see a play by Lope de Vega, you should go to:

    a el concierto   **b** el teatro

3   If you want to listen to some relaxing music, you should go to:

    a el club de jazz   **b** el club nocturno

4   If you want to see a movie, you should go to:

    a el teatro   **b** el cine

Activity B

List your three favorite places to go at night.

1   _____

2   _____

3   _____

Activity C

Listen to where each person wants to go this evening, and write the place in the blank.

1   Yazid quiere ir _____.

2   Sofía quiere ir _____.

3   Federico quiere ir _____.

4   Lucía quiere ir _____.

5   Claudio quiere ir _____.

Activity D

Label the following places.

1   _____

2   _____

3   _____

4   _____

LESSON 3

Smart Phrases

Core Phrases

Yo amo…	I like…
la música clásica	classical music
la música pop	pop music
el jazz	jazz
el rap	rap
el rock	rock music
la música española	Spanish music

¿Me puede recomendar un concierto?	Can you recommend a concert?
¿Cuándo comienza/termina el concierto?	When does the concert begin/end?
¿Cuánto tiempo dura?	How long does it last?
¿Cuánto cuesta el boleto?	How much is a ticket?

CULTURE TIP

If you want to see a concert or play while you're in Spain, you can see schedules and buy tickets at some of the larger stores such as *Fnac* or *Corte Inglés*.

Activity A

Say what kind of music each person likes.

1 Reinaldo ama Chopin, Beethoven y Debussy.

_____

2 Carlota y Martín aman Ana Torroja, Miguel Bosé y Joaquín Sabina.

_____

3 Nosotros amamos Louis Armstrong, Dizzie Gillespie y Ella Fitzgerald.

_____

Activity B

Fill in the blanks with the correct Spanish word.

1 ¿Cuánto _____ dura?

2 ¿_____ cuesta el boleto?

3 ¿Me puede _____ un concierto?

Activity C

Write the question associated with each answer.

_____

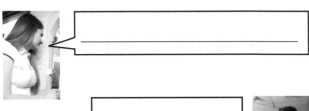
Cuesta 15€ el boleto.

_____

El concierto dura dos horas.

_____

El concierto termina a las 10:00.

LESSON 4

Smart Grammar

The prepositions *a* and *de*

In general, the preposition *a* means "to" and *de* means "from" when used before places and events. They often precede definite articles (*el, la, los, las*) and form contractions as follows:

	a	de
m sing.	al	del
f sing.	a la	de la
pl.	a los/las	de los/las

For example:

Jaime va a la fiesta.	Jaime is going to the party.
Reinaldo va al concierto.	Reinaldo is going to the concert.
Ana María regresa del cine.	Ana Maria is coming back from the movie theater.
Martina regresa de las vacaciones.	Martina is returning from vacation [holiday].

SMART TIP

Don't forget to use the preposition *a* to talk about going to cities and *de* to talk about coming from cities. For example, if you want to say that you're from New York, say *Yo soy de Nueva York.*

Activity A

Choose the correct answer.

1 Nosotros vamos _____ café.
   a al   **b** del

2 Tú vas _____ Granada.
   a a la   **b** a

3 Ustedes vienen _____ Segovia.
   a a   **b** de

4 Ellos van _____ iglesia.
   a a la   **b** al

Activity B

Complete the sentences with the correct preposition. Don't forget to use the correct contraction when necessary.

1 Tristán va _____ museo.

2 Antonio y Laura regresan _____ café.

3 Pablo va _____ Ibiza.

4 Miguel regresa _____ teatro.

Activity C

¿Adónde quiere ir usted? Write down 3 different places or monuments you want to visit. Make sure you use the correct preposition!

1 _____

2 _____

3 _____

Activity D

Write the correct form of the preposition and article.

1 Antonio y Susana van _____ museo.

2 Cristina viene _____ fiesta.

3 Martín regresa _____ casa.

4 Ustedes van _____ monumento.

5 Juan y José salen _____ bares.

LESSON 5

¿Adónde ir?

Where to go?

In many larger cities in Spain you can find weekly magazines that list all the concerts, movies and events for that week. Here's an example of the kinds of shows you might find.

Viernes

16:00 – **Concierto de Jazz**
Centro Comercial ParqueSur
Entrada gratis

Carmina Burana
Auditorio Nacional de Música
15€ el boleto

20:00 – **Concierto de Rock**
La Boca del Lobo, Madrid
15€ el boleto

Concierto de Pop
Teatro Lara, Madrid
15€, 1 bebida gratis

Sábado

19:00 – **Las cuatro estaciones de Vivaldi**
Auditorio Nacional de la Música
15€ el boleto

Calígula
Teatro Fernán Gómez, Centro de Arte
Entrada gratis

21:00 – **La Loba (Pop-Rock)**
Café La Palma
10€, 1 bebida gratis

Activity A

Fabio has had a long week and he needs to get out this weekend, but he only has 60€ to spend. He likes rock music, rap and classical plays. Where can he go, and how much money will he spend?

1 _____

2 _____

3 _____

Total: _____ €

Activity B

Which three activities/events would you choose?

1 _____

2 _____

3 _____

SMART TIP

If an event or museum is labeled *entrada gratis*, it means that there is no charge for entry. You may still need a ticket, however, so make sure you check.

Activity C

Listen to each character and select the correct answer based on the events listed in the magazine.

1

a El concierto es en el Café La Palma.

b El concierto es a las 11:00 (23:00).

2

a El concierto es en el Auditorio Nacional de Música.

b El concierto es en La Boca del Lobo.

3

a Cuesta 15€ el boleto.

b Es a las 20:00.

LESSON 6 — Words to Know

Core Words

el bar	bar (inside a club)
el/la barista	bartender (m/f)
la bebida	drink
la botella	bottle
el disk jockey	DJ
el guardarropa	coat check
el guardia	bouncer
la pista de baile	dance floor

CULTURE TIP

Many clubs in Spain offer you a drink with the cover charge. For example, you may see a sign: *Entrada 20€, 1 bebida gratis* (Cover charge 20€, 1 free drink).

Activity A

Write in Spanish where each person is.

1

_____

2

_____

3

_____

Activity B

Write the job of each person in Spanish.

1

_____

2

_____

3

_____

Activity C

Choose the correct answer.

1 To check your coat, go to:
  a el guardia
  b el guardarropa

2 If you want a drink, go to:
  a el bar
  b la bebida

3 If you want to dance, go to:
  a la pista de baile
  b la botella

4 When you enter the club you have to pay:
  a el precio de entrada
  b el disc jockey

5 If you get a free drink with the cover charge, it's called a:
  a bebida gratis
  b bebida de entrada

LESSON 7

Smart Phrases

Core Phrases

¿Te puedo invitar a una bebida?	Can I buy you a drink?
¡Encantado!/¡Encantada!	With pleasure! (m/f)
¿Quieres bailar?	Do you want to dance?
¿Hay alguien aquí?	Is someone sitting here? (lit. "Is someone here?")
No, no hay nadie.	No, there's nobody here.
¿Les interrumpí?	Am I interrupting?
¿Me puedo sentar con ustedes?	Can I join you?
¿A qué te dedicas?	What do you do for a living?
Yo trabajo para _____.	I work for _____.
Yo soy estudiante.	I'm a student.
Yo estoy jubilado/ jubilada.	I'm retired. (m/f)

SMART TIP

If you're in a bar or club setting, people often use the informal *tú* or *vosotros(as)* instead of *usted* or *ustedes*. For example, someone might say *¿Te puedo invitar a una bebida?* or *¿Queréis bailar?*

Activity A

Write three ways to strike up a conversation with a stranger.

1 _____

2 _____

3 _____

Activity B

How do you ask...

1 ...if the seat is taken?

_____

2 ...if you can join someone?

_____

3 ...if you're interrupting?

_____

4 ...if you can buy someone a drink?

_____

Activity C

Write the logical question for each answer.

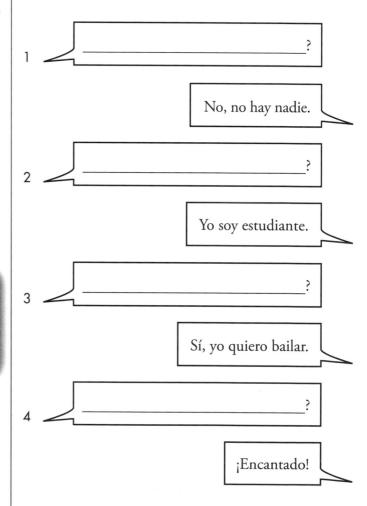

1 _____ ?

No, no hay nadie.

2 _____ ?

Yo soy estudiante.

3 _____ ?

Sí, yo quiero bailar.

4 _____ ?

¡Encantado!

LESSON 8
Smart Grammar

The verbs *decidir* (to decide) and *salir* (to go out)

To conjugate the verbs *decidir* and *salir* in the present tense, remove the *–ir* ending and add the following endings:

	decidir	to decide
yo	decido	I decide
tú	decides	you decide
usted	decide	you decide
él/ella	decide	he/she decides
nosotros/nosotras	decidimos	we decide
vosotros/vosotras	decidís	you decide
ustedes	deciden	you decide
ellos/ellas	deciden	they decide

	salir	to go out
yo	salgo	I go out
tú	sales	you go out
usted	sale	you go out
él/ella	sale	he/she goes out
nosotros/nosotras	salimos	we go out
vosotros/vosotras	salís	you go out
ustedes	salen	you go out
ellos/ellas	salen	they go out

Activity A
Fill in the blanks with the correct form of the verb *decidir*.

1 Nosotros _____ a dónde ir la próxima semana (next week).

2 Ellos _____ a dónde ir de vacaciones.

3 Yo _____ llevar a mi familia (family).

4 Él _____ ir en coche (car).

5 Tú _____ qué hacer el fin de semana.

6 ¿Adónde _____ ir con sus amigos?

7 Ella _____ hacer un crucero.

Activity B
Fill in the blanks with the correct form of the verb *salir*.

1 Beatriz y Camila _____ a un club nocturno.

2 Ella _____ con Juan Carlos.

3 Vosotros _____ tarde.

4 ¿Quieres _____ esta noche (this evening)?

5 Yo _____ a cenar.

6 Nosotros _____ juntos (together).

7 Él _____ al club nocturno con nosotros.

Activity C
Answer the questions in Spanish.

1 ¿Salen tarde ustedes?

_____

2 ¿Adónde salen esta noche?

_____

3 ¿Deciden ustedes salir de vacaciones con su familia o sin su familia?

_____

4 ¿Salen ustedes con su familia a Mallorca?

_____

Activity D
Choose the correct answer.

1 Nosotros _____ de vacaciones.
   a decidimos   b salimos

2 Ella _____ a un bar.
   a decide   b sale

3 Yo _____ ir a Finisterra para las vacaciones.
   a decido   b salgo

4 Ellos _____ a un club nocturno.
   a deciden   b salen

Unit 9 Review

Activity A
List three different places where you can go at night.

1 _____
2 _____
3 _____

Activity B
Select the correct preposition for each sentence.

1 Felipe va _____ concierto de jazz.

   a a un   **b** a

2 Sandra va _____ Sevilla.

   a a la   **b** a

3 Teresa entra _____ cine.

   a del   **b** al

Activity C
Complete the crossword puzzle.

Across

  3 to dance
  4 drink
  5 theater

Down

  1 movie theater
  2 vacation
  3 bottle

Activity D
Select the logical answer for each question.

1 ¿Cuánto tiempo dura?

   a El concierto dura una hora y media.

   b Yo amo la música española.

2 ¿Quieres bailar?

   a ¡Encantada!

   b No puedo quedarme hasta muy tarde.

3 ¿Cuánto cuesta el boleto?

   a El concierto comienza a las 7:00.

   b Son 20€ el boleto.

Activity E
Complete the verb charts.

	salir	decidir
yo		
tú		
usted		
él/ella		
nosotros/nosotras		
vosotros/vosotras		
ustedes		
ellos/ellas		

Challenge
Can you conjugate the verbs *decidir* and *salir* out loud without writing them down?

Internet Activity
Want to see what's happening in Madrid this week? How about Barcelona? Go online to **www.berlitzbooks.com/5Mtravel** to find links to some of the best event guides in Spain. Try to find some events that interest you.

Unit 10 Health & Resources

In this unit you will learn:
- how to ask for help.
- what to say at the doctor's office.
- different parts of the body.
- reflexive verbs and the past tense with *haber*.

LESSON 1

¡Socorro!

Dialogue

It's *las 11:00 de la noche* (11 o'clock at night) and Ana is looking for an all-night pharmacy. She has just stopped a passing *policía* (police officer) to ask for help.

Ana	Perdone, ¿podría usted ayudarme?
Policía	Sí, señora.
Ana	Busco la farmacia que está abierta toda la noche.
Policía	No está lejos de aquí.
Ana	¿Podría usted indicarme el camino?
Policía	Tome usted la cuarta calle a la izquierda y la farmacia está a su derecha.
Ana	¡Muchas gracias!
Policía	De nada.

Activity A

Circle **T** for True and **F** for False.

1 Ana busca una farmacia.   **T / F**
2 Ana habla con un policía.   **T / F**
3 La farmacia no está abierta toda la noche.   **T / F**
4 La farmacia no está lejos.   **T / F**

SMART TIP

Stores that are open all night are *abierto/abierta toda la noche* or *abierto/abierta 24 horas*.

Activity B

Imagine you are looking for an all-night pharmacy. Complete the conversation with the police officer.

¿Le puedo ayudar?

_____ Usted

No está lejos de aquí.

_____ Usted

Tome usted la cuarta calle a la izquierda y la farmacia está a su derecha.

_____ Usted

LESSON 2

Words to Know

Core Words

el bombero	firefighter
la comisaría	police station
el consultorio	doctor's office
el enfermero/ la enfermera	nurse (m/f)
el hospital	hospital
el médico/la médica	doctor (m/f)
el policía	police officer
la sala de urgencia	emergency room [casualty department]

CULTURE TIP

If you need to call for help in Spain, dial 061 for medical, 092 for local police and 080 for fire. Note that often firefighters respond to medical emergencies.

Activity A

Write who to call along with the phone number if there is a…

1   …fire.

_____ (_____)

2   …medical emergency.

_____ (_____)

3   …theft.

_____ (_____)

Activity B

Label each person.

1 _____   2 _____

3 _____   4 _____

Activity C

Label each place.

1 _____   2 _____

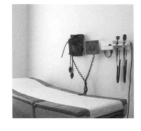

3 _____

LESSON 3

Smart Phrases

Core Phrases

¡Fuego!	Fire!
¡Socorro!	Help!
¡Ladrón!	Thief!
¡Me han robado!	I've been robbed!
¡Cuidado!	Watch out!
Me he roto el brazo/ la pierna.	I broke my arm/ my leg.
Soy…	I am…
asmático/asmática	asthmatic (m/f)
diabético/diabética	diabetic (m/f)
Estoy enfermo/enferma.	I am sick. (m/f)

Activity A

What should you say if…

1 …you are robbed?

_____

2 …there is a fire?

_____

3 …you need help?

_____

4 …someone is going to trip and fall?

_____

5 …you broke your leg?

_____

6 …you are diabetic?

_____

Activity B

Write what each person would say to describe his or her ailment.

1 _____

2 _____

3 _____

4 _____

Activity C

Unscramble the letters and write the correct phrases.

1 r o s o r c o   _ _ _ _ _ _ _

2 g e o f u   _ _ _ _ _

3 i u c o d a d   _ _ _ _ _ _ _

4 o r a l d n   _ _ _ _ _ _

Activity D

Match the English expressions with their Spanish equivalents.

1	Fire!	**a**	¡Cuidado!
2	Watch out!	**b**	¡Ladrón!
3	Help!	**c**	¡Fuego!
4	Thief!	**d**	¡Socorro!

SMART TIP

When something is passing, you use the verb *estar* to describe it, for example *Tú estás enfermo*, "You are sick," and *Nosotros estamos tristes*, "We are sad." On the other hand, when something is chronic or permanent, you use the verb *ser*, for example, *Yo soy disléxico*, "I am dyslexic," and *Yo soy amoroso*, "I am loving."

Smart Grammar

SMART TIP
To form the negative with a reflexive verb, add *no* before the reflexive pronoun. For example, *Él no se viste,* "He doesn't get dressed."

Reflexive Verbs

Reflexive verbs are used when the subject is performing the action on himself, herself or itself. They take two steps to conjugate. First, you must use the correct reflexive pronoun for each person, placing it before the verb, and then conjugate the verb following regular conjugation patterns. For example, take the reflexive verb *acostarse* (to go to bed).

yo	**me**	acuesto	I go to bed
tú	**te**	acuestas	you go to bed
usted	**se**	acuesta	you go to bed
él/ella	**se**	acuesta	he/she goes to bed
nosotros/ nosotras	**nos**	acostamos	we go to bed
vosotros/ vosotras	**os**	acostáis	you go to bed
ustedes	**se**	acuestan	you go to bed
ellos/ellas	**se**	acuestan	they go to bed

Here are some other reflexive verbs:

cepillarse (el cabello/los dientes)	to brush (one's hair/teeth)
despertarse	to wake up
divertirse	to enjoy oneself
ducharse	to take a shower
lavarse	to wash oneself
levantarse	to get up
llamarse	to call oneself/to be named
pasearse	to take a walk
razurarse	to shave
reposarse	to rest
romperse (el brazo/la pierna)	to break (one's arm/leg)
sentirse	to feel
vestirse	to get dressed

Activity A
Fill in the blanks with the correct reflexive pronoun.

1 Él _____ llama Jerónimo.

2 Nosotros _____ paseamos.

3 Tú _____ levantas a las 5:00 de la mañana.

4 Usted _____ reposa.

Activity B
Write what is happening in each picture.

1 Jean _____.

2 Annie _____.

3 Él _____.

Activity C
Match the personal pronoun with the correct reflexive pronoun.

1	yo	a	nos
2	nosotros	b	os
3	ellas	c	se
4	vosotros	d	te
5	tú	e	me

LESSON 5

La salud

Dialogue

Jim has a *fiebre* (fever) and is feeling *enfermo* (sick) while on vacation. Listen to his conversation with *el médico* (the doctor).

El médico	¿Qué le pasa?
Jim	Yo me siento enfermo.
El médico	¿Cuáles son sus síntomas?
Jim	Tengo fiebre y me duele la cabeza.
El médico	¿Tiene tos?
Jim	Sí, y también me duele la garganta.
El médico	Yo pienso que usted tiene la gripe.
Jim	¿Qué me aconseja usted?
El médico	Usted debe reposar y beber mucha agua.

SMART TIPS

- If something hurts you, say *Me duele el/la...* followed by the body part that hurts. For example, *Me duele la garganta* means "My throat hurts."
- The verb *toser*, "to cough," is a regular –er verb.

Activity A

Circle **T** for True and **F** for False.

1 Jim está enfermo. **T / F**

2 El médico piensa que él tiene la gripe. **T / F**

3 Jim tiene que reposarse. **T / F**

4 Jim tiene que beber mucho vino. **T / F**

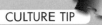

CULTURE TIP

Even if you don't benefit from the Spanish *seguridad social* (national health insurance), it can be relatively inexpensive to see a doctor while in Spain. Just note that you will be expected to pay up front.

Activity B

Check off Jim's symptoms.

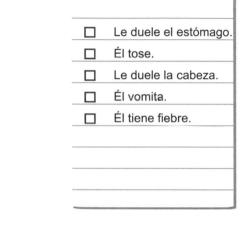

☐	Le duele el estómago.
☐	Él tose.
☐	Le duele la cabeza.
☐	Él vomita.
☐	Él tiene fiebre.

Activity C

How do you say…

1 …you have a headache?

_____

2 …you feel sick?

_____

3 …you have the flu?

_____

4 …you have a sore throat?

_____

Your Turn

Imagine that you're at a doctor's office with the flu. Practice describing your symptoms to the doctor.

LESSON 6

Words to Know

Core Words

El cuerpo (Body)

el brazo	arm
la cabeza	head
el dedo	finger
la espalda	back
el estómago	stomach
la garganta	throat
el hombro	shoulder
la mano	hand
el pecho	chest
el pie	foot
la pierna	leg
la rodilla	knee

La cara (Face)

la boca	mouth
el cabello	hair
el diente	tooth
la lengua	tongue
la nariz	nose
el ojo	eye
la oreja	ear

SMART TIP

Spanish has some words that are feminine but end with o, like *la mano* "the hand."

Activity A

Label the parts of the face in Spanish.

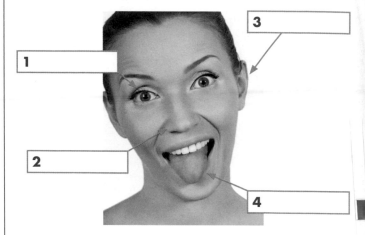

Activity B

Label the parts of the body in Spanish.

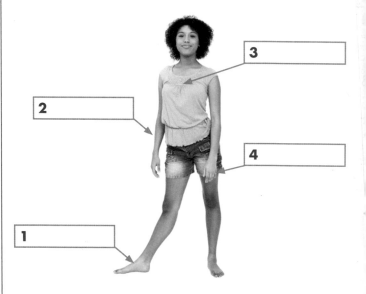

Activity C

Complete the word webs with parts of *el cuerpo* or *la cara*.

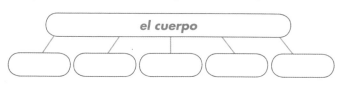

Smart Phrases

Core Phrases

Yo quisiera…	I would like…
un antiácido	antacids
unas aspirinas	aspirin
una crema protectora contra el sol	sunscreen
un acetaminofén	acetaminophen [paracetamol]
un jarabe para la tos	cough syrup
unas pastillas para la garganta	throat lozenges
unas vendas	bandages [plasters]

¿Qué me recomienda usted para…?	What do you recommend for…?
un catarro	a cold
el dolor de estómago	stomach pains
la indigestión	indigestion
la gripe	the flu
el mareo	motion sickness
la nausea	nausea
la tos	a cough

Usted necesita una receta médica.	You need a prescription.

CULTURE TIP

Pharmacies are easy to spot in Spain; they all display a green cross outside, which is often lit by neon. If you need a pharmacy, just follow the flashing green lights.

Activity A

Circle the items that can be purchased at *la farmacia*.

- pan
- pastillas para la garganta
- vendas
- zapatos
- antiácidos
- aspirinas
- boletos

Activity B

Write the medicine that each person needs.

1 A Natalia le duele la garganta.

_____

2 A David le duele la cabeza.

_____

3 Sandra tiene una tos fuerte.

_____

Activity C

How do you ask what the pharmacist recommends for…

1 …nausea?

_____

2 …a cold?

_____

3 …motion sickness?

_____

**Smart
Grammar**

- To use the negative in the past tense, place the *no* before the conjugated verb *haber*. For example, *Yo no he perdido mi pasaporte*, "I didn't lose my passport."
- Some of the verbs you have already learned have irregular past participles:

abrir	→ abierto	poner	→ puesto
decir	→ dicho	resolver	→ resuelto
escribir	→ escrito	romper	→ roto
hacer	→ hecho	ser	→ sido
imprimir	→ impreso	volver	→ vuelto

Past tense using *haber*

To form the past tense, *el pasado compuesto*, in Spanish you use the verb *haber*. The present tense of *haber* is followed by the past participle of the verb.

Regular *-ar* verbs

To form the past participle of regular *-ar* verbs, drop the *-ar* ending and add *-ado*.

		viajar	**to travel**
yo	he	viajado	I have traveled
tú	as	viajado	you have traveled
usted	ha	viajado	you have traveled
él/ella	ha	viajado	he/she has traveled
nosotros/ nosotras	hemos	viajado	we have traveled
vosotros/ vosotras	habéis	viajado	you have traveled
ustedes	han	viajado	you have traveled
ellos/ellas	han	viajado	they have traveled

Regular *-ir* verbs

To form the past participle of regular *-ir* verbs, drop the *-ir* ending and add *-ido*.

		dormir	**to sleep**
yo	he	dormido	I have slept
tú	has	dormido	you have slept
usted	ha	dormido	you have slept
él/ella	ha	dormido	he/she has slept
nosotros/ nosotras	hemos	dormido	we have slept
vosotros/ vosotras	habéis	dormido	you have slept
ustedes	han	dormido	you have slept
ellos/ellas	han	dormido	they have slept

Regular *-er* verbs

To form the past participle of regular *-er* verbs, drop the *-er* ending and add *-ido*.

		perder	**to lose**
yo	he	perdido	I have lost
tú	has	perdido	you have lost
usted	ha	perdido	you have lost
él/ella	ha	perdido	he/she has lost
nosotros/ nosotras	hemos	perdido	we have lost
vosotros/ vosotras	habéis	perdido	you have lost
ustedes	han	perdido	you have lost
ellos/ellas	han	perdido	they have lost

Activity A

Answer the following questions in the past tense.

1 ¿Ha visitado usted el Museo Arqueológico Nacional?

_____

2 ¿Ha pedido usted un postre?

_____

3 ¿Ha contestado usted el teléfono?

_____

4 ¿Ha comprado usted un vestido?

_____

5 ¿Ha hecho usted sus maletas?

_____

Activity A
How do you say…

1   …someone stole your wallet?

_____

2   …"Help!"?

_____

3   …you broke your leg?

_____

4   …your feet hurt?

_____

5   …your throat hurts?

_____

Activity B
Describe each person.

1   Teófilo _____.

2   Lucía _____.

3   Mateo _____.

4   Anita _____.

Activity C
Check off symptoms of *la gripe*.

☐   Me duele la cabeza.

☐   Tengo fiebre.

☐   Me duele la rodilla.

☐   Me duele la garganta.

☐   Me siento mareado.

☐   Tengo una tos fuerte.

Activity D
Put the following sentences in the *pasado compuesto*.

1   Yo viajo con mi familia.

_____

2   Nosotros escogemos el almuerzo.

_____

3   Ellas comen una torta.

_____

4   Él no contesta el teléfono.

_____

5   Tú miras la tele.

_____

Challenge
Stand in front of a mirror and point to and name at least 10 parts of your body or face.

Internet Activity
Go online to **www.berlitzbooks.com/5Mtravel** to find tips on how to have a safe trip in Spain and then make a list of 5 things you can do to keep safe.

Unit 11 Heading Home

In this unit you will learn how to:
- talk about family members.
- use comparatives.
- describe your trip.
- form the past tense using *ser*.

LESSON 1

Queridos amigos

La tarjeta postal

Ryan is at the end of his trip and wants to *enviar* (send) some postcards to his Spanish-speaking *amigos* (friends) at home. Read his message to Susana and answer the questions that follow.

Querida Susana,

Yo me divierto en Barcelona. Es una ciudad hermosa y yo he hecho muchas cosas. He visitado el Museo de Arte Moderno y la Catedral gótica. Yo he hablado con muchos españoles. Ellos son muy majos. También hay buenos restaurantes y ¡he comido mucho!

¡Hasta pronto!
Ryan

Susana Rodríguez
305 Oak Street
Princeton, NJ 08540
ESTADOS UNIDOS

Activity B

Ryan leaves tomorrow. Check off what he's done already to find out what he still needs to do today.

PARA HACER

_____ visitar el Museo de Arte Moderno

_____ visitar la fuente mágica de Montjuic

_____ hablar con los españoles

_____ comer mucho

_____ ver un espetáculo

_____ visitar la Catedral gótica

Activity C

Practice writing your own postcard.

Activity A

Fill in the missing words from Ryan's postcard.

1 Yo _____ en Barcelona.

2 Yo he _____ muchas cosas.

3 He _____ el Museo de Arte Moderno y la Catedral gótica.

4 Yo he _____ con muchos españoles.

5 Hay buenos restaurantes y ¡he _____ mucho!

SMART TIP

A typical greeting for letters and postcards to good friends is *Querido* (m), *Querida* (f), *Queridos* (m pl.) or *Queridas* (f pl.), which all mean "Dear…."

CULTURE TIP

Don't forget that stamps can be bought at the post office and at *tabaquerías*. Once your postcard is ready to go, drop it at the post office or in one of the yellow mailboxes you can find on the street. In larger cities, there will be one slot for local mail labeled *Dentro de Madrid* (Inside Madrid) and another slot labeled *Fuera de Madrid* (Outside Madrid).

Words to Know

Core Words

el marido	husband
la mujer	wife
el compañero/la compañera	partner (m/f)
los niños	children
el hijo	son
la hija	daughter
los padres	parents
el papá	father
la mamá	mother
el hermano	brother
la hermana	sister
el abuelo	grandfather
la abuela	grandmother
el nieto	grandson
la nieta	granddaughter
el tío	uncle
la tía	aunt
el sobrino	nephew
la sobrina	niece
el primo/la prima	cousin (m/f)

SMART TIP

Here are some adjectives you might need to know to talk about your family members:

alto/alta	tall (m/f)
bajo/baja	short (m/f)
bello/bella	beautiful (m/f)
feo/fea	ugly (m/f)
jóven	young
viejo/vieja	old (m/f)

Activity A

Choose the correct picture for each underlined word.

1 Tomás quiere comprar una camisa para su <u>papá</u>.

2 Luis quiere enviar una tarjeta postal a su <u>hijo</u>.

3 Lauriano quiere viajar con su <u>hermana</u>.

4 Silvia quiere comprar un recuerdo para su <u>abuela</u>.

Activity B

Don't forget to bring home some souvenirs! Write what you want to buy for each of the following people:

1 mis padres _____

2 mis hijos _____

3 mi tío _____

4 mi prima _____

5 mi compañero/
  mi compañera _____

LESSON 3
Smart Phrases

Core Phrases

¡Nos vemos pronto!	See you soon!
¡Hasta la próxima!	See you next time!
Ha sido un placer.	It was a pleasure.
Me he divertido.	I had a great time.
Gracias por su gentileza/hospitalidad.	Thank you for your kindness/hospitality.
Estamos en contacto.	Let's keep in touch.
Te voy a extrañar.	I'm going to miss you.

SMART TIP

To say, "I miss you" in Spanish, you say *Te extraño*, but you can also say *Me haces falta*, literally, "You are missing to me."

Activity A
How do you say…

1 …you want to keep in touch?

_____

2 …you had a great time?

_____

3 …you're going to miss the other person?

_____

4 …you hope to see the other person soon?

_____

5 …it was a pleasure?

_____

Activity B
Fill in the missing words from the phrases and arrange the circled letters to find a bonus word.

1 ¡Hasta la ⬭___ __ __ __ __ __!

2 Gracias por tu __ __ __ __ ⬭ __ __ __
__ __ __ __ __.

3 Te voy a __ __ __ __ ⬭ __ __ __.

4 Estamos en ⬭__ __ __ __ __ __ __.

5 Me he __ __ __ ⬭ __ __ __ __ __
mucho.

6 ¡Nos vemos __ ⬭ __ __ __ __!

Bonus word: __ __ __ __ __ __

Activity C
Write the Spanish equivalent of each phrase.

1
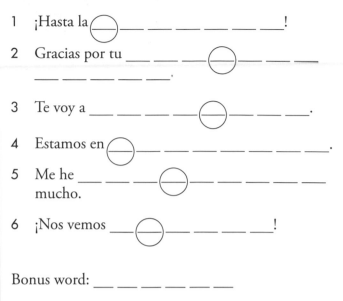
See you next time!

2

It was a pleasure.

3

I'm going to miss you.

- If something is better or worse, use the comparatives *mejor* (better) and *peor* (worse). For example, *El hotel de cuatro estrellas* (stars) *es mejor que el hotel de dos estrellas*, "The four-star hotel is better than the two-star hotel."

- Make sure that the adjective agrees with the first noun. For example, *Ella es más alta que su hermano*, "She is taller than her brother."

Los comparativos (Comparatives)

There are three ways to form comparatives in Spanish when they are used with adjectives:

Superiority: *más... que*

Madrid es más grande que Quito.	Madrid is bigger than Quito.

Inferiority: *menos... que*

El tren es menos rápido que el avión.	The train is slower than the plane. (Literally, The train is less fast than the plane.)

Equality: *tan... como*

Mi hermano es tan alto como mi papá.	My brother is as tall as my father.

Activity A

Use the words below to create your own comparative sentences.

1 mi papá, mi mamá

_____

2 el español, el inglés

_____

3 el pastel, la ensalada

_____

4 vino, cerveza

_____

5 mi abuela, mi mamá

_____

Activity B

Compare the following people and items.

1

Mateo   Marco

Marco es _____ alto que Mateo.

2

La camisa es _____ cara como los zapatos.

3

| ■ Madrid | 20°C |
| ■ Barcelona | 25°C |

Hace _____ calor en Madrid que en Barcelona.

Activity C

Choose the logical comparative for the following sentences.

1 Barcelona es _____ grande que Vigo.

2 La ensalada cuesta _____ cara como el filete.

3 Está _____ caliente en Egipto como en Rusia.

4 El restaurante de tres estrellas es _____ que el restaurante de dos estrellas.

LESSON 5
¡Adiós!

Dialogue

Ryan has just finished packing his bags and he's saying goodbye to his colleague Juan.

Juan	¿Ha hecho las maletas?
Ryan	Sí, estoy listo para salir.
Juan	¿Le ha gustado la ciudad?
Ryan	Me ha encantado la ciudad. Es más bella que la mía.
Juan	¿Ha visitado varios lugares?
Ryan	Sí, y he comprado muchos recuerdos para mi familia.
Juan	Ha sido un placer verle.
Ryan	¡Adiós! ¡Nos vemos pronto!

SMART TIP

In Spanish, as in English, there are two ways to refer to something that is yours. You can say *Ésta es mi maleta,* "This is my suitcase," or *Esta maleta es mía,* "This suitcase is mine." However if you are referring to your city, flight, train, etc. you can only say it one way: *Esta es mi ciudad,* "This is my town," *Este es mi vuelo,* "This is my flight," *Este es mi tren,* "This is my train."

Activity A

Circle **T** for true or **F** for false.

1	Juan ha hecho sus maletas.	T / F
2	Ryan no está listo para salir.	T / F
3	A Ryan le ha encantado la ciudad.	T / F
4	Ryan ha visitado varios lugares.	T / F

Activity B

Imagine you are saying goodbye to Juan. Complete the dialogue.

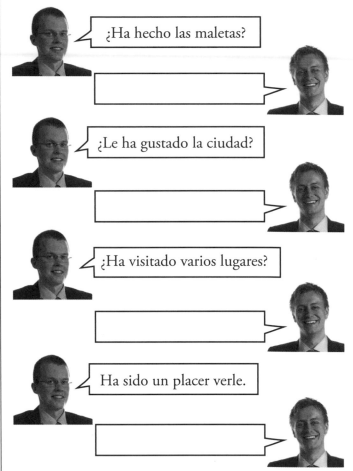

¿Ha hecho las maletas?

¿Le ha gustado la ciudad?

¿Ha visitado varios lugares?

Ha sido un placer verle.

Activity C

Answer the questions based on the dialogue in Spanish.

1 ¿Ha hecho Ryan sus maletas?

_____

2 ¿Le ha gustado a Ryan la ciudad?

_____

3 ¿Ha visitado Ryan varios lugares?

_____

4 ¿Ha comprado Ryan muchos regalos?

_____

Words to Know

Core Words

aburrido/aburrida	boring (m/f)
delicioso/deliciosa	delicious (m/f)
divertido/divertida	fun (m/f)
espantoso/espantosa	scary (m/f)
extraño/extraña	strange (m/f)
genial	fantastic [brilliant]
horrible	horrible
horroroso	awful, dreadful
increíble	incredible
interesante	interesting
magnífico/magnífica	magnificent (m/f)
romántico/romántica	romantic (m/f)

SMART TIPS

- When describing how something was in the past, use the imperfect tense of *ser* and *estar*. For example, *¡La cena estaba increíble!* "The dinner was incredible!" or *¡Las montañas eran inmensas!* "The mountains were enormous!"

- Sometimes there is a very subtle difference between *ser* and *estar*. For example, in *El hotel estaba hermoso para la fiesta*, the word *heromoso* means it was beautiful at that time, while in *El hotel era hermoso*, the word *hermoso* was a characteristic of the hotel.

Activity A

Write 5 sentences to describe a current or past vacation [holiday].

1 _____
2 _____
3 _____
4 _____
5 _____

Activity B

Fill in the blanks with the correct adjective. Make sure it agrees with the noun!

1 El museo estaba _____.
interesting

2 Las piezas estaban _____.
boring

3 La ciudad es muy _____.
romantic

4 La comida en el hotel estaba _____.
awful

5 El viaje en avión estaba _____.
scary

Activity C

List four *buenos* (good) adjectives and four *malos* (bad).

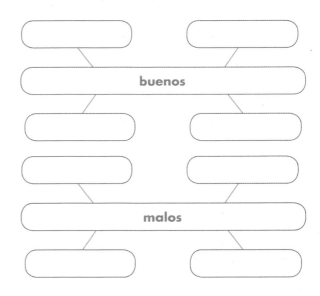

buenos

malos

Your Turn

Use your new vocabulary to describe your best vacation ever and your worst vacation ever.

LESSON 7

Smart Phrases

Core Phrases

Yo he ido a España.	I have gone to Spain.
¡Ha sido el mejor viaje de mi vida!	It was the best trip of my life!
Toda la gente ha sido muy amable.	Everyone has been very nice.
Yo he hecho muchos amigos	I made a lot of friends.
Estoy loco/loca por…	I can't wait to… (m/f)
salir	leave
ir a casa	go home
volver	go back
regresar	come back
ver las fotos	see the pictures
volverte a ver	see you again
Yo me quiero quedar más tiempo.	I want to stay longer.
Yo me he divertido mucho.	I have had a great time.
Me he quedado allí _____ días/semanas/meses.	I stayed there for _____ days/weeks/months.

Activity A

How do you say…

1   …you stayed there for 6 days?

_____

2   …you went to Spain?

_____

3   …you can't wait to see the pictures?

_____

4   …you can't wait to go back?

_____

Activity B

Did these people have a good time on their vacation?

1

¡Estoy loco por volver!

a   Él se ha divertido mucho.
b   Él no se ha divertido mucho.

2

Estoy loca por salir.

a   Ella se ha divertido mucho.
b   Ella no se ha divertido mucho.

3

¡Nosotros nos queremos quedar más tiempo!

a   Ellos se han divertido mucho.
b   Ellos no se han divertido mucho.

Activity C

Answer the questions in Spanish.

1   ¿Has ido tú a España?

_____

2   ¿Ha hecho usted muchos amigos?

_____

3   ¿Ha sido amable toda la gente?

_____

SMART TIP

In Spanish when you love a place and can't wait to go back you say *Estoy loco por volver*, "I can't wait to go back" (literally, I'm crazy to return).

LESSON 8

Smart Grammar

The *presente continuo* tense using *estar*

The *presente continuo* tense expresses the idea of being in the process of doing something: *Ellos están viajando a Londres.* (They are traveling to London.)

To form the present continuous use the verb *estar* in the present tense followed by the gerund of the main verb. The gerund is formed by dropping the *–ar* and replacing it with *–ando*, or replacing the *–er* or *–ir* with *–iendo*.

		entrar	to enter
yo	estoy	entrando	I am entering
tu	estás	entrando	you are entering
usted	está	entrando	you are entering
él/ella	está	entrando	he/she is entering
nosotros/ nosotras	estamos	entrando	we are entering
vosotros/ vosotras	estáis	entrando	you are entering
ustedes	están	entrando	you are entering
ellos/ellas	están	entrando	they are entering

Don't forget to use the reflexive pronouns when using reflexive verbs in the *presente continuo*.

Ella <u>se</u> está vistiendo.   She is getting dressed.

SMART TIP

For many irregular verbs, you need to learn what the gerund is. For example, *caer/cayendo, ir/yendo, leer/leyendo, venir/viniendo, vestir/vistiendo.*

Activity A

Rewrite the following sentences in the *presente continuo*.

1 Ellos se quedan tres días en Mallorca.

_____

2 Ella llega a las tres de la mañana.

_____

3 Él se divierte.

_____

4 Yo vengo con mi familia.

_____

5 Nosotros vamos al aeropuerto.

_____

Activity B

Fill in the blanks with the verbs in the *presente continuo*.

1 Felipe _____ (go down) las escaleras.

2 Ellas _____ (go) de vacaciones.

3 Manuel _____ (eat) un filete.

4 Nosotros _____ (make) las maletas.

5 Tú _____ (go up) a tu cuarto.

Activity C

Write the correct gerund for each verb.

venir	
salir	
quedar	
llegar	
leer	
bajar	
pasar	
caer	
nacer	

Your Turn

Imagine that you are telling your new Spanish friends what are your plans for the day. Use the present continuous to tell as many activities as you can.

Activity A

Write a postcard to a Spanish friend telling him or her about your recent vacation.

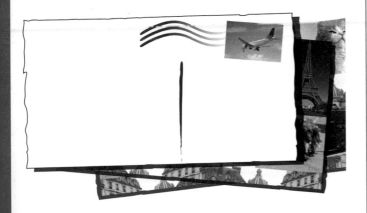

Activity B

Compare the people in the following pictures.

Lola   Mateo

1 Mateo es _____ que Lola.

La princesa

La bruja

2 La bruja es _____ que la princesa.

Ramón   Ana

3 Ramón está _____ que Ana.

Activity C

Circle the correct answer.

1 ¿Quién es la mamá de mi hermana?
   a mi tía   b mi mamá

2 ¿Quién es el hijo de mi tío?
   a mi hermano   b mi primo

3 ¿Quién es el papá de mi papá?
   a mi nieto   b mi abuelo

4 ¿Quién es la hija de mi papá?
   a mi prima   b mi hermana

Activity D

Answer the following questions about your vacation.

1 ¿Se está divirtiendo?

_____

2 ¿Adónde está yendo hoy?

_____

3 ¿En dónde se está quedando?

_____

4 ¿Cuánto tiempo se está quedando allí?

_____

5 ¿Cuándo están saliendo de viaje?

_____

Challenge

Can you conjugate the verbs *comprar*, *divirtierse* and *venir* in the *presente continuo*?

Internet Activity

Want to send some online cards or postcards in Spanish? Go to **www.berlitzbooks.com/5Mtravel** for a list of websites where you can send your friends and family *tarjetas postales virtuales*.

Spanish–English Glossary

A

a la derecha	ah lah deh-<u>reh</u>-chah	to the right
a la izquierda	ah lah eez-kee-<u>ehr</u>-dah	to the left
el abono	ehl ah-<u>boh</u>-noh	booklet (of tickets)
el abrigo	ehl ah-<u>bree</u>-goh	n coat
abrir	ah-<u>breer</u>	v to open
la abuela	lah ah-<u>bweh</u>-lah	grandmother
el abuelo	ehl ah-<u>bweh</u>-loh	grandfather
aburrido/ aburrida	ah-boo-<u>ree</u>-doh/ ah-boo-<u>ree</u>-dah	boring (m/f)
el acceso	ehl ahk-<u>seh</u>-soh	n access (m)
el acceso a Internet de alta velocidad	ehl ahk-<u>seh</u>-soh ah een-tehr-<u>net</u> deh ahl-tah beh-loh-see-<u>dahd</u>	high-speed Internet access (m)
el acetaminofén	ehl ah-she-tah-mee-noh-<u>fen</u>	acetaminophen [paracetamol] (m)
acostarse	ah-kohs-<u>tahr</u>-seh	v to go to bed
el adaptador	ehl ah-dahp-tah-<u>dohr</u>	adapter (m)
la aduana	lah ah-<u>dwah</u>-nah	customs
el aeropuerto	ehl ah-eh-roh-<u>pwehr</u>-toh	airport (m)
la agencia de viajes	lah ah-<u>khehn</u>-see-ah deh-<u>byah</u>-khes	travel agency (f)
el agua	ehl <u>ah</u>-gwah	still water
el agua mineral	ehl <u>ah</u>-gwah mee-neh-<u>rahl</u>	sparkling water
el aire acondicionado	ehl <u>ahee</u>-reh ah-kohn-dee-syoh-<u>nah</u>-doh	air conditioning
al final de	ahl fee-<u>nahl</u> deh	at the end of
al frente	ahl <u>frehn</u>-teh	across from
al lado de	ahl <u>lah</u>-doh deh	next to
el alemán	ehl ah-leh-<u>mahn</u>	n German (language)
Alemania	ah-leh-<u>mah</u>-nee-ah	Germany (f)
alérgico/ alérgica a	ah-<u>lehr</u>-khee-koh/ ah-<u>lehr</u>-khee-kah ah	allergic to (m/f)
los almacenes	lohs ahl-mah-<u>sehn</u>-ehs	department store
la almohada	lah ahl-<u>mwah</u>-dah	pillow (m)
el almuerzo	ehl ahl-<u>mwehr</u>-soh	lunch
aló	ah-<u>loh</u>	hello (when answering the phone)
amar	ah-<u>mahr</u>	v to love
amarillo/amarilla	ah-mah-<u>ree</u>-yoh/ ah-mah-<u>ree</u>-yah	yellow (m/f)
americano/ americana	ah-meh-ree-<u>kah</u>-noh/ ah-meh-ree-<u>kah</u>-nah	adj American (m/f)
anaranjado/ anaranjada	ah-nah-rahn-<u>khah</u>-doh/ ah-nah-rahn-<u>khah</u>-dah	orange (m/f)
andar	ahn-<u>dahr</u>	v to walk
el año	ehl <u>ah</u>-nyoh	year (m)
antes	<u>ahn</u>-tehs	before
el antiácido	ehl ahn-tee-<u>ah</u>-see-doh	antacid (m)
la antigüedad	lah ahn-tee-gweh-<u>dahd</u>	n antique (f)
apagar	ah-pah-<u>gahr</u>	v to turn off
el aparato	ehl ah-pah-<u>rah</u>-toh	machine, device (m)
el apellido	ehl ah-peh-<u>yee</u>-doh	last name
el aperitivo	ehl ah-peh-ree-<u>tee</u>-boh	cocktail/before-dinner drink (m)
aprender	ah-prehn-<u>dehr</u>	v to learn
el archivo	ehl ahr-<u>chee</u>-boh	n file
arreglar	ah-rreh-<u>glahr</u>	to clean (the room)
el ascensor	ehl ah-sehn-<u>sohr</u>	elevator [lift] (m)
el asiento	ehl ah-<u>syehn</u>-toh	seat
asmático(a)	ahs-<u>mah</u>-tee-koh/ ahs-<u>mah</u>-tee-kah	asthmatic
la aspirina	lah ah-spee-<u>ree</u>-nah	aspirln (f)
atravesar	ah-trah-beh-<u>sahr</u>	to cross
Australia	ah-oo-<u>strah</u>-lee-ah	Australia (f)
australiano/ australiana	ah-oo-strah-lee-<u>ah</u>-noh/ ah-oo-strah-lee-<u>ah</u>-nah	adj Australian (m/f)
el autobús	ehl ah-oo-toh-<u>boos</u>	bus
el avión	ehl ah-<u>byohn</u>	airplane (m)
ayer	ah-<u>yehr</u>	yesterday
ayudar	ah-yoo-<u>dahr</u>	v to help
azul	ah-<u>sool</u>	blue

B

bailar	bah-ee-<u>lahr</u>	v to dance
bajar/bajarse	bah-<u>khahr</u>/bah-<u>khahr</u>-seh	v to go down, to get off
el banco	ehl <u>bahn</u>-koh	n bank
la bañera	lah bah-<u>nyeh</u>-rah	tub
el baño completo	ehl <u>bah</u>-nyo kohm-<u>pleh</u>-toh	bathroom (with tub or shower)
los baños	lohs <u>bah</u>-nyohs	bathroom (f)
el bar	ehl bahr	bar
el/la barista	ehl/lah bar-<u>ees</u>-tah	bartender (m/f)
beber	beh-<u>behr</u>	v to drink
la bebida	lah beh-<u>bee</u>-dah	n drink
bello/bella	<u>beh</u>-yoh/<u>beh</u>-yah	adj beautiful (m/f)
la bici, la bicicleta	lah <u>bee</u>-see, lah bee-see-<u>kleh</u>-tah	bicycle
bien	byehn	well
bien cocido	byehn koh-<u>see</u>-doh	well-done
bienvenido/ bienvenida	byehn-beh-<u>nee</u>-doh/ byehn-beh-<u>nee</u>-dah	welcome
el billete	ehl bee-<u>yeh</u>-teh	ticket, bill
la billetera	lah bee-yeh-<u>teh</u>-rah	wallet
blanco/blanca	<u>blahn</u>-koh/<u>blahn</u>-kah	white (m/f)
la boca	lah <u>boh</u>-kah	mouth
la boleta de venta	lah boh-leh-tah deh behnta	receipt
el boleto	ehl boh-<u>leh</u>-toh	ticket
el boleto de embarque	ehl boh-<u>leh</u>-toh deh ehm-<u>bahr</u>-keh	boarding pass

adj adjective   v verb   adv adverb   n noun

Spanish–English Glossary

el bolso	ehl bohl-soh	handbag
el bombero	ehl bohm-beh-roh	firefighter
bonito/bonita	boh-nee-toh/boh-nee-tah	pretty (m/f)
borrar	boh-rrahr	v to delete
el bote	ehl boh-teh	boat
la botella (de vino)	lah boh-teh-yah deh bee-noh	bottle (of wine)
la boutique	lah boo-teek	store [shop]
el brazo	ehl brah-soh	arm
buenas noches	bweh-nahs noh-chehs	good night
buenas tardes	bweh-nahs tahr-dehs	good evening
bueno/buena	bweh-noh/bweh-nah	good (m/f)
buenos días	bweh-nohs dee-ahs	hello
el bus	ehl boos	bus
buscar	boo-skahr	v to look for

C

el cabello	ehl kah-beh-yoh	hair
la cabeza	lah kah-beh-sah	head
caer	kah-ehr	v to fall
el café	ehl kah-feh	coffee
la caja	lah kah-khah	cash register
la caja de chocolates	lah kah-khah deh choh-koh-lah-tehs	box of chocolates
el cajero automático	ehl kah-kheh-roh ahoo-toh-mah-tee-koh	ATM
la calle	lah kah-yeh	street
la cama	lah kah-mah	bed
la cama doble	lah kah-mah doh-bleh	double bed
la cama individual	lah kah-mah een-dee-bee-dwahl	single bed
el camarón	ehl kah-mah-rohn	shrimp
cambiar	kahm-byahr	v to change
el cambio	ehl kahm-byo	n change
caminar	kah-mee-nahr	v to take a walk
caminar	kah-mee-nahr	v to walk
Canadá	kah-nah-dah	Canada
canadiense	kah-han-dyehn-she	adj Canadian
cancelar	kahn-seh-lahr	v to cancel
la carne	lah kahr-neh	meat
la carne de res	lah kahr-neh deh rehs	beef
caro/cara	kah-roh/kah-rah	expensive (m/f)
el carrito para equipaje	ehl kah-rree-toh-pah-rah eh-kee-pah-kheh	baggage cart
la carta	lah kahr-tah	menu
el castillo	ehl kah-stee-yoh	castle
el catarro	ehl kah-tah-rroh	n cold
el celular	ehl seh-loo-lahr	cell phone [mobile]
la cena	lah seh-nah	dinner
el centavo	ehl sehn-tah-boh	cent
el centro comercial	ehl sehn-troh koh-mehr-syahl	n mall
cerca de	sehr-kah deh	close to
el cerdo	ehl sehr-doh	pork
cerrar	seh-rrahr	v to close
la cerveza	lah sehr-beh-sah	beer
el champú	ehl chahm-poo	n shampoo
la chaqueta	lah chah-keh-tah	n jacket
el cheque de viajero	ehl cheh-keh deh vyah-kheh-roh	traveler's check
el chocolate caliente	ehl choh-koh-lah-teh kah-lyehn-teh	hot chocolate
el cibercafé	ehl see-behr-kah-feh	Internet café
el cigarillo	ehl see-gah-ree-yoh	cigarette
el cine	ehl see-neh	movie theater
el cinturón	ehl seen-too-rohn	n belt
el club de jazz	ehl klub deh jas	jazz club
el club nocturno	ehl kloob nok-toor-noh	night club
la coca	lah koh-kah	cola
la coca de dieta	lah koh-kah deh dyeh-tah	diet cola
el coche	ehl koh-cheh	car
comenzar	koh-mehn-sahr	to begin
comer	koh-mehr	v to eat
la comida	lah koh-mee-dah	meal
la comisaría	lah koh-mee-sah-reeyah	police station
cómo	koh-moh	how
cómodo/cómoda	koh-moh-doh/koh-moh-dah	adj comfortable (m/f)
el compañero/ la compañera	ehl kohm-pah-nyeh-roh/ lah kohm-pah-nyeh-rah	partner (m/f)
comprar	kohm-prahr	v to buy
comprender	kohm-prehn-dehr	v to understand
la computadora	lah kohm-poo-tah-dohr-ah	computer (m)
la computadora portátil	lah kohm-poo-tah-dohr-ah pohr-tah-teel	laptop (m)
con	kohn	with
con dirección a	kohn dee-rek-syon ah	in the direction of
el concierto	ehl kohn-syehr-toh	concert
conecter	koh-nek-tahr	v to connect
el consultorio	ehl kohn-sool-toh-ree-oh	doctor's office
la contraseña	lah kohn-trah-seh-nya	password
la corbata	lah kohr-bah-tah	n necktie
el cordero	ehl kohr-deh-roh	lamb (m)
el correo	ehl koh-rreh-oh	post office
el correo electrónico	ehl koh-rreh-oh eh-lek-troh-nee-koh	n e-mail
costar	kohs-tahr	cost
la crema protectora contra el sol	lah kreh-mah proh-tek-toh-rah kohn-trah ehl sohl	sunscreen

adj adjective　　　v verb　　　adv adverb　　　n noun

Spanish–English Glossary

el crucero	ehl kroo-<u>seh</u>-roh	cruise
el cuadro	ehl <u>kwa</u>-droh	painting
cuánto/cuántos	<u>kwahn</u>-toh/<u>kwahn</u>-tohs	how much/how many
la cuchara	lah koo-<u>chah</u>-rah	spoon
el cuchillo	ehl koo-<u>chee</u>-yoh	knife
la cuenta	lah <u>kwehn</u>-tah	n check (f)
cuidado	kwee-<u>dah</u>-doh	careful
la cuna	lah <u>koo</u>-nah	crib

D

dar	dahr	v to give
de nada	deh <u>nah</u>-dah	you're welcome
de paso	deh <u>pah</u>-soh	passing through
decidir	deh-see-<u>deer</u>	to decide
decir	deh-<u>seer</u>	v to say
declarar	deh-klah-<u>rahr</u>	v to declare
el dedo	ehl <u>deh</u>-doh	finger
delante de	deh-<u>lahn</u>-teh deh	in front of
deletrear	deh-leh-treh-<u>ahr</u>	v to spell
delicioso/ deliciosa	deh-lee-<u>syoh</u>-soh/ deh-lee-<u>syoh</u>-sah	delicious (m/f)
dentro de	<u>dehn</u>-troh deh	in
el desayuno	ehl deh-sah-<u>yoo</u>-noh	breakfast
descargar	dehs-kahr-<u>gahr</u>	v to download
el descuento	dehs-<u>kwehn</u>-toh	n discount
despertarse	dehs-pehr-<u>tahr</u>-seh	v to wake up
después	dehs-<u>pwehs</u>	after
detrás de	deh-<u>trahs</u> deh	behind
devolver	deh-bohl-<u>behr</u>	return (give back)
el día	ehl <u>dee</u>-ah	day
diabético/ diabética	dyah-<u>beh</u>-tee-koh/ dyah-<u>beh</u>-tee-kah	adj diabetic (m/f)
el dibujo	ehl dee-<u>boo</u>-khoh	drawing
el diente	ehl <u>dyehn</u>-teh	tooth
el digestivo	ehl dee-kheh-<u>stee</u>-boh	liqueur/ after-dinner drink
la dirección	lah dee-rek-<u>syohn</u>	n address (f)
el disk jockey	ehl deesk <u>joh</u>-keh-ee	DJ
divertido/ divertida	dee-behr-<u>tee</u>-doh/ dee-behr-<u>tee</u>-dah	fun (m/f)
divertirse	dee-behr-<u>teer</u>-seh	v to enjoy oneself
el dólar	ehl <u>doh</u>-lahr	dollar
el dolor de estómago	ehl doh-<u>lohr</u> deh eh-<u>stoh</u>-mah-goh	stomach pain
ducharse	doo-<u>chahr</u>-seh	v to take a shower

E

los efectos personales	lohs eh-<u>fek</u>-tohs pehr-soh-<u>nah</u>-lehs	personal belongings (m)
elegir	eh-leh-<u>kheer</u>	v to choose
ella	<u>eh</u>-yah	she, it
ellos/ellas	<u>eh</u>-yohs/<u>eh</u>-yahs	they (m/f pl.)
en casa de	ehn <u>kah</u>-sah deh	at the house of
en dónde	ehn <u>dohn</u>-deh	where
en efectivo	ehn eh-fek-<u>tee</u>-boh	n cash
en línea	ehn <u>lee</u>-nyah	online
en	ehn	in/on
encantado/ encantada	ehn-kahn-<u>tah</u>-doh/ ehn-kahn-<u>tah</u>-dah	with pleasure (m/f)
encontrar	ehn-kohn-<u>trahr</u>	v to find
el enfermero/ la enfermera	ehl ehn-fehr-<u>meh</u>-roh/ lah ehn-fehr-meh-rah	nurse (m/f)
enfermo/enferma	ehn-<u>fehr</u>-moh/ ehn-<u>fehr</u>-mah	sick (m/f)
engordar	ehn-gohr-<u>dahr</u>	v to gain weight/get fat
el enlace	ehl ehn-<u>lah</u>-seh	n link
la ensalada	lah ehn-sah-<u>lah</u>-dah	salad
entender	ehn-tehn-<u>dehr</u>	v to understand
la entrada	lah ehn-<u>trah</u>-dah	entry, appetizer (f)
entrar	ehn-<u>trahr</u>	v to enter
enviar	ehn-<u>byahr</u>	v to send, to ship
envolver	ehm-bohl-<u>behr</u>	v to wrap
el equipaje	ehl eh-kee-<u>pah</u>-kheh	luggage, baggage
el equipaje de mano	ehl eh-kee-<u>pah</u>-kheh	hand luggage
equivocado	eh-kee-boh-<u>kah</u>-doh	mistaken
la escala	lah eh-<u>skah</u>-lah	stopover (f)
la escalera	lah eh-skah-leh-rah	staircase, step
escoger	eh-skoh-<u>khehr</u>	v to choose
escribir	eh-skree-<u>beer</u>	v to write
el escritorio	ehl es-kree-<u>toh</u>-ree-oh	desk
escuchar	eh-skoo-chahr	v to listen
la espalda	lah ehs-<u>pahl</u>-dah	back
España	ehs-<u>pah</u>-nyah	Spain (f)
el español	ehl ehs-pah-<u>nyohl</u>	n Spanish (language)
español/ española	ehs-pah-<u>nyohl</u>/ ehs-pah-nyoh-lah	adj Spanish (m/f)
espantoso/ espantosa	ehs-spahn-<u>toh</u>-soh/ ehs-spahn-<u>toh</u>-sah	scary (m/f)
esperar	eh-speh-<u>rahr</u>	v to wait (for)
esquiar	ehs-<u>kyahr</u>	v to go skiing
los Estados Unidos	lohs ehs-<u>tah</u>-dohs oo-<u>nee</u>-dohs	United States (m)
estar	eh-<u>stahr</u>	v to be
el estómago	ehl eh-<u>stoh</u>-mah-goh	stomach
el estudiante/ la estudiante	ehl ehs-too-<u>dyahn</u>-teh/ lah ehs-too-<u>dyahn</u>-teh	student (m/f)
el euro	ehl <u>eh</u>-oo-roh	euro (m)
extraño/extraña	ehks-<u>trah</u>-nyoh/ ehks-<u>trah</u>-nyah	strange (m/f)

adj adjective	v verb	adv adverb	n noun

F

la factura	lah fahk-too-rah	receipt
el farmacéutico/ la farmacéutica	ehl fahr-mah-seh-oo-tee-koh/ lah fahr-mah-seh-oo-tee-kah	pharmacist (m/f)
la farmacia	lah fahr-mah-syah	pharmacy
la fecha	lah feh-chah	date
feo/fea	feh-oh/feh-ah	ugly (m/f)
la fiesta	lah fyehs-tah	party
el filete	ehl fee-leh-teh	steak
el flan	ehl flahn	vanilla pudding
la floristería	lah floh-rees-teh-ree-ah	flower shop
el francés	ehl frahn-sehs	n French (language)
francés/francesa	frahn-sehs/frahn-seh-sah	adj French (m/f)
Francia	frahn-syah	France
la fruta	lah froo-tah	fruit
el fuego	ehl fweh-goh	fire
fumador	foo-mah-dohr	smoking
funcionar	foon-syohn-ahr	to work

G

la garganta	lah gahr-gahn-tah	throat
gastar	gahs-tahr	v to spend (money)
genial	kheh-nyahl	fantastic [brilliant]
grande	grahn-deh	big
gratuito	grah-twee-toh	free
la gripe	lah gree-peh	flu
gris	grees	gray
guardar	gwahr-dahr	v to save
el guardarropa	ehl gwahr-dah-rroh-pah	coat check
el guardia	ehl gwahr-dyah	bouncer (m/f)
gustarle	goos-tahr-leh	to like

H

haber	ah-behr	to have
la habitación	lah ah-bee-tah-syohn	room
hablar	ah-blahr	v to speak
hacer	ah-sehr	v to do/to make
hacer click	ah-sehr kleek	v to click
hacer compras	ah-sehr kohm-prahs	to shop
hacer deporte	ah-sehr deh-pohr-teh	to do sports
hacer falta	ah-sehr fahl-tah	v to miss
hacer fila	ah-sehr fee-lah	to stand in line
hacer surfing	ah-sehr soor-feeng	v to go surfing
hacia	ah-syah	toward
hasta luego	ahs-tah lweh-goh	goodbye
la hermana	lah ehr-mah-nah	sister
el hermano	ehl ehr-mah-noh	brother
hermoso/hermosa	ehr-moh-soh/ehr-moh-sah	adj beautiful (m/f)
la hija	lah ee-khah	daughter

el hijo	ehl ee-khoh	son
hola	oh-lah	hi
el hombre	ehl ohm-breh	man (m)
el hombro	ehl ohm-broh	shoulder (m)
la hora	lah oh-rah	time (f)
el horario	ehl oh-rah-ryoh	schedule (m)
horrible	oh-rree-bleh	awful, dreadful (m/f)
horroroso	oh-rroh-roh-soh	horrible
el hospital	ehl oh-spee-tahl	hospital (m)
hoy	oh-eey	today

I

la iglesia	lah ee-gleh-syah	church (f)
la impresora	lah eem-preh-soh-rah	printer (f)
imprimir	eem-pree-meer	v to print
los impuestos de aduana	lohs eem-pweh-stohs deh ah-dwah-nah	customs duty (m)
increíble	een-kreh-ee-bleh	incredible
indicar el camino	een-dee-kahr ehl kah-mee-noh	v to give directions
la indigestión	lah een-dee-khehs-tyohn	indigestion (f)
Inglaterra	een-glah-teh-rrah	England (f)
el inglés	ehl een-glehs	n English (language) (m)
inglés/inglesa	een-glehs/een-gleh-sah	adj English (m/f)
las instrucciones	lahs eens-trook-syoh-nehs	directions (f)
interesante	een-teh-reh-sahn-teh	interesting
el Internet	ehl een-tehr-net	Internet (m)
ir	eer	v to go
Italia	ee-tah-lyah	Italy (f)
el italiano	ehl ee-tah-lyah-noh	n Italian (language) (m)
italiano/italiana	ee-tah-lyah-noh/ ee-tah-lyah-nah	adj Italian (m/f)

J

el jabón	ehl khah-bohn	soap
el jarabe para la tos	ehl khah-rah-beh pah-rah lah tohss	cough syrup
la jarra de agua	lah khah-rrah deh ah-gwah	pitcher of water
el jazz	ehl jas	jazz
el jean	ehl jeen	n jeans
joven	khoh-behn	young
la joya	lah khoh-yah	piece of jewelry
la joyería	lah khoh-yeh-ree-ah	jewelry store [jeweller's]
jubilado/jubilada	khoo-bee-lah-doh/ khoo-bee-lah-dah	retired (m/f)
el jugo de naranja	ehl khoo-goh deh nah-rahn-khah	orange juice
el juguete	ehl khoo-geh-teh	toy

adj	adjective		v	verb	adv adverb	n	noun

L

el ladrón	ehl lah-<u>drohn</u>	n thief
el lavabo	ehl lah-<u>bah</u>-boh	sink
lavarse	lah-<u>bahr</u>-seh	v to wash oneself
la leche	lah <u>leh</u>-cheh	milk
leer	leh-<u>ehr</u>	v to read
leer el correo electrónico	leh-<u>ehr</u> ehl koh-<u>rreh</u>-oh eh-lek-<u>troh</u>-nee-koh	v to check e-mail
la lengua	lah <u>lehn</u>-gwah	language, tongue
lentamente	lehn-tah-<u>mehn</u>-teh	slowly
levantar el auricular	leh-bahn-<u>tahr</u> ehl ah-oo-ree-koo-<u>lahr</u>	v to pick up the phone
levantarse	leh-bahn-<u>tahr</u>-seh	v to get up
la libra	lah <u>lee</u>-brah	pound
la librería	lah lee-breh-<u>ree</u>-ah	bookstore
el libro	ehl <u>lee</u>-broh	book
la limosina	lah lee-moh-<u>see</u>-nah	shuttle
limpio/limpia	<u>leem</u>-pyoh/<u>leem</u>-pyah	adj clean (m/f)
lindo/linda	<u>leen</u>-doh/<u>leen</u>-dah	adj beautiful (m/f)
llamarse	yah-<u>mahr</u>-seh	v to call oneself/ to be named
la llave	lah <u>yah</u>-beh	key
el llavero	ehl ya-<u>beh</u>-roh	keychain
las llegadas	lahs yeh-<u>gah</u>-dahs	arrivals (f)
llegar	yeh-<u>gahr</u>	v to arrive
lograr	loh-<u>grahr</u>	v to succeed
el lugar de nacimiento	ehl loo-<u>gahr</u> deh nah-see-<u>myen</u>-toh	place of birth

M

la madre	lah <u>mah</u>-dreh	mother
la madrugada	lah mah-droo-<u>gah</u>-dah	before dawn
magnífico/ magnífica	mahg-<u>nee</u>-fee-koh mahg-<u>nee</u>-fee-kah	magnificent (m/f)
la maleta	lah mah-<u>leh</u>-tah	suitcase
malo/mala	<u>mah</u>-loh/<u>mah</u>-lah	bad (m/f)
mañana	mah-<u>nyah</u>-nah	tomorrow
la mano	lah <u>mah</u>-noh	hand
la manta	lah <u>mahn</u>-tah	blanket
marcar el número	mahr-<u>kahr</u> ehl <u>noo</u>-meh-roh	v to dial the number
el mareo	ehl mah-<u>reh</u>-oh	motion sickness
el marido	ehl mah-<u>ree</u>-doh	husband
marrón	mah-<u>rrohn</u>	brown
más	mahss	more
la mascada	lah mahs-<u>kah</u>-dah	scarf (f)
el medicamento	ehl meh-dee-kah-<u>mehn</u>-toh	medicine
la medicina	lah meh-dee-<u>see</u>-nah	medicine
el médico/ la médica	ehl <u>meh</u>-dee-koh/ lah <u>meh</u>-dee-kah	doctor (m/f)

el mejillón	ehl meh-khee-<u>yohn</u>	mussel
mejor	meh-<u>khohr</u>	best
la memoria de USB	lah meh-<u>moh</u>-ryah deh oo-eh-seh-<u>beh</u>	USB key/flash drive
menos	<u>meh</u>-nohs	less
el mensaje nuevo	ehl mehn-<u>sah</u>-kheh <u>nweh</u>-voh	new message
el menú	ehl meh-<u>noo</u>	prix-fixe menu
el mercado	ehl mehr-<u>kah</u>-doh	market
el mes	ehl mehss	month
el metro	ehl <u>meh</u>-troh	subway
la moda	lah <u>moh</u>-dah	fashion
modificar	moh-dee-fee-<u>kahr</u>	v to modify
molestar	moh-leh-<u>stahr</u>	v to bother, disturb
la moneda	lah moh-<u>neh</u>-dah	coin
el montañismo	ehl mohn-tah-<u>nyees</u>-moh	v to go hiking
el monumento	ehl moh-noo-<u>mehn</u>-toh	monument
morado/morada	moh-<u>rah</u>-doh/moh-<u>rah</u>-dah	purple (m/f)
morir	moh-<u>reer</u>	v to die
mostrar	mohs-<u>trahr</u>	v to show
la movilidad reducida	moh-bee-lee-<u>dahd</u> reh-doo-<u>see</u>-dah	handicapped
mucho	<u>moo</u>-choh	a lot
la mujer	lah moo-<u>khehr</u>	woman, wife
el municipio	ehl moo-nee-<u>see</u>-pyoh	town hall [council]
el museo	ehl moo-<u>seh</u>-oh	museum
la música	lah <u>moo</u>-see-kah	music

N

nacer	nah-<u>sehr</u>	v to be born
la nacionalidad	lah nah-syoh-nah-lee-<u>dahd</u>	nationality
nada	<u>nah</u>-dah	nothing
la nariz	lah nah-<u>rees</u>	nose
negro/negra	<u>neh</u>-groh/<u>neh</u>-grah	black (m/f)
la nieta	lah <u>nyeh</u>-tah	granddaughter
el nieto	ehl <u>nyeh</u>-toh	grandson
el niño/la niña	ehl <u>nee</u>-nyoh/lah <u>nee</u>-nyah	child (m/f)
no fumador	noh foo-mah-<u>dohr</u>	non-smoking
no molestar	noh moh-leh-<u>stahr</u>	do not disturb
el nombre	ehl <u>nohm</u>-breh	first name
nosotros/nosotras	noh-<u>soh</u>-trohs/noh-<u>soh</u>-trahs	we (m/f)
nuevo/nueva	<u>nweh</u>-voh/<u>nweh</u>-vah	new (m/f)
el número	ehl <u>noo</u>-meh-roh	number

O

el official de aduana	ehl oh-fee-<u>syahl</u> deh ah-<u>dwah</u>-nah	customs officer
la oficina de cambio de divisas	lah oh-fee-<u>see</u>-nah deh <u>kam</u>-byoh deh dee-<u>bee</u>-sahs	currency exchange office

adj adjective	v verb	adv adverb	n noun

las oficinas de turismo	las oh-fee-<u>see</u>-nahss deh too-<u>rees</u>-moh	tourism office (m)
oír	oh-eer	to hear
el ojo	ehl <u>oh</u>-khoh	eye (m)
el ordenador	ehl orh-deh-nah-<u>dohr</u>	computer (m)
el ordenador portátil	ehl orh-deh-nah-<u>dohr</u> pohr-<u>tah</u>-teel	laptop (m)
la oreja	lah oh-<u>reh</u>-khah	ear (f)

P

los padres	lohs <u>pah</u>-drehs	parents
pagar	pah-gahr	to pay
el pan	ehl pahn	bread
la panadería	lah pahn-ah-deh-<u>ree</u>-ah	bakery
la pantalla	lah pahn-<u>tah</u>-yah	screen (f)
el pantalón	pahn-tah-<u>lohn</u>	n pants
el papel higiénico	ehl pah-<u>pehl</u> ee-khyehn-ee-koh	toilet paper
la parada de taxis	lah pah-<u>rah</u>-dah deh tahks-ees	taxi stand [rank]
el parque	ehl <u>pahr</u>-keh	n park
partir	pahr-<u>teer</u>	v to leave
el pasaporte	ehl pah-sah-<u>pohr</u>-teh	passport
pasar	pah-<u>sahr</u>	v to pass
pasarlo	pah-<u>sahr</u>-loh	pass him (tel.)
el pastel	ehl pah-<u>stehl</u>	cake
la pastilla	lah pah-<u>stee</u>-ya	throat lozenge
el pato	ehl <u>pah</u>-toh	duck
el peaje	ehl peh-<u>ah</u>-kheh	toll booth
el pecho	ehl <u>peh</u>-choh	chest
pedir	peh-<u>deer</u>	v to ask (for)
peinarse	pey-<u>nahr</u>-seh	v to brush
pensarlo	pehn-<u>sahr</u>-loh	v to think about something
peor	peh-<u>ohr</u>	worst
pequeño/ pequeña	peh-<u>keh</u>-nyoh/ peh-keh-nyah	small (m/f)
perder	pehr-<u>dehr</u>	v to lose
perdido/perdida	pehr-<u>dee</u>-doh/pehr-<u>dee</u>-dah	lost (m/f)
perdone	pehr-<u>doh</u>-neh	excuse me
el perfume	ehl pehr-<u>foo</u>-meh	perfume
el periódico	ehl peh-<u>ryoh</u>-dee-koh	newspaper
permanecer	pehr-mah-neh-sehr	v to stay, to remain
el pescado	ehl peh-<u>skah</u>-doh	n fish
el pie	ehl pee-<u>eh</u>	foot
la pierna	lah <u>pyehr</u>-nah	leg
el piso	ehl <u>pee</u>-soh	floor (m)
la pista de baile	lah <u>pees</u>-tah deh <u>bah</u>-ee-leh	dance floor
la plancha	lah <u>plahn</u>-chah	n iron
la planta	lah <u>plahn</u>-tah	floor (m)
la planta baja	lah <u>plahn</u>-tah <u>bah</u>-khah	ground floor
poder	poh-<u>dehr</u>	v to be able to
el policía	ehl poh-lee-<u>see</u>-ah	police officer
la policía	lah poh-lee-<u>see</u>-ah	police
el pollo	ehl <u>poh</u>-yoh	chicken
por favor	por fah-<u>bohr</u>	please
por qué	pohr-<u>keh</u>	why
el postre	ehl <u>poh</u>-streh	dessert
el precio completo	ehl <u>preh</u>-see-oh kohm-<u>pleh</u>-toh	full price
el precio de entrada	ehl <u>preh</u>-syoh deh ehn-<u>trah</u>-dah	cover charge
preguntar	preh-goon-<u>tahr</u>	to ask
prender	prehn-<u>dehr</u>	v to turn on
presionar	preh-syoh-<u>nahr</u>	v to type, to press
el primo/ la prima	ehl <u>pree</u>-moh/ lah <u>pree</u>-mah	cousin
los productos de belleza	lohs proh-<u>dook</u>-tohs deh beh-<u>yeh</u>-sah	beauty products (m pl.)
la propina	lah proh-<u>pee</u>-nah	n tip
el propósito	ehl proh-<u>poh</u>-see-toh	purpose, goal
próximo/ próxima	<u>prok</u>-see-moh/ <u>prok</u>-see-mah	next (m/f)
el puente	ehl <u>pwehn</u>-teh	bridge
la puerta	lah <u>pwehr</u>-tah	gate

Q

querer	keh-<u>rehr</u>	v to want
el queso	ehl <u>keh</u>-soh	cheese
quitar	kee-<u>tahr</u>	v to remove

R

el rap	ehl rap	rap
rasurarse	rah-soo-<u>rahr</u>-seh	v to shave
el ratón	ehl rah-<u>tohn</u>	mouse
recargar	reh-kahr-<u>gahr</u>	to refill
la receta	lah reh-<u>seh</u>-tah	prescription (f)
el recibo	ehl reh-see-boh	receipt
recomendar	reh-koh-mehn-<u>dahr</u>	v to recommend
recto	<u>rehk</u>-toh	straight ahead
la región	lah reh-<u>khyohn</u>	region
registrarse	reh-khee-<u>strahr</u>-seh	n check-in (m)
renovar	reh-noh-vahr	v to renew
repetir	reh-peh-teer	v to repeat
reposarse	reh-poh-<u>sahr</u>-seh	v to rest
la reserva, la reservación	la reh-sehr-vah, lah reh-sehr-bah-<u>syohn</u>	reservation
reservar	reh-sehr-vahr	v to reserve
responder	rehss-pohn-dehr	v to answer

adj adjective   v verb   adv adverb   n noun

Spanish	Pronunciation	English
el retiro de equipaje	ehl reh-tee-roh deh eh-kee-pah-kheh	baggage claim
el rock	ehl rok	rock music
la rodilla	lah roh-dee-yah	knee
rojo/roja	roh-khoh/roh-khah	red (m/f)
romántico/ romántica	roh-mahn-tee-koh/ roh-mahn-tee-kah	romantic (m/f)
romperse	rohm-pehr-seh	v to break
rosado/rosada	roh-sah-doh/roh-sah-dah	pink (m/f)

S

la sala de urgencia	lah sah-lah deh oor-khehn-syah	emergency room [casualty department] (f pl.)
la salida	lah sah-lee-dah	n exit
salir	sah-leer	v to go out
el salmón	ehl sahl-mohn	salmon
la secadora de pelo	lah seh-kah-doh-rah deh peh-loh	hairdryer
la semana	lah seh-mah-nah	week
sentir	sehn-teer	v to feel
ser	sehr	v to be
el servicio	ser-bee-syoh	service
el servicio de lavandería	ehl sehr-bee-syoh deh lah-bahn-deh-ree-ah	laundry service
la servilleta	lah sehr-bee-yeh-tah	napkin
servir	sehr-beer	v to serve
siguiente	see-gyehn-teh	next
la silla	lah see-yah	chair
simpático/ simpática	seem-pah-tee-koh/ seem-pah-tee-kah	nice
sin	seen	without
el sitio Web	ehl see tyoh web	website
sobre	soh-breh	on
la sobrina	lah soh-bree-nah	niece
el sobrino	ehl soh-bree-noh	nephew
solamente, sólo	soh-lah-mehn-teh, soh-loh	only, just
la sopa	lah soh-pah	soup
el souvenir, el recuerdo	ehl soo-beh-neer, ehl reh-kwehr-doh	souvenir
subir	soo-beer	v to go up, to get on
sucio/sucia	soo-syoh/soo-syah	dirty (m/f)
el suéter	ehl sweh-tehr	sweater
el supermercado	ehl soo-pehr-mehr-kah-doh	supermarket

T

la tabaquería	lah tah-bah-keh-ree-ah	tobacco shop [smoke shop]
también	tahm-bee-ehn	also
la tapería	lah tah-peh-ree-ah	tapas restaurant
tarde	tahr-deh	late
la tarde	lah tahr-deh	afternoon
la tarjeta de crédito	lah tahr-kheh-tah deh kreh-dee-toh	credit card
la tarjeta postal	lah tahr-khe-tah poh-stahl	postcard
la tarjeta telefónica	lah tahr-kheh-tah teh-leh-foh-nee-kah	n phone card
la tarta	lah tahr-tah	pie
la tasa de cambio	lah tah-sah deh kahm-byoh	exchange rate
el taxi	ehl tahk-see	taxi
la taza	lah tah-sah	cup/mug
el té	ehl teh	tea
el té helado	ehl teh eh-lah-doh	iced tea
el teatro	ehl teh-ah-troh	theater [theatre]
el teclado	ehl teh-klah-doh	keyboard
la tele/ la televisión	lah teh-leh/la teh-leh-bee-syohn	television
el teléfono	ehl teh-leh-foh-noh	n telephone
el tenedor	ehl teh-neh-dohr	fork
tener	teh-nehr	v to have
tener calor	teh-nehr kah-lohr	v to be hot
tener frío	teh-nehr free-oh	v to be cold
tener hambre	teh-nehr ahm-breh	v to be hungry
tener miedo	teh-nehr myeh-doh	v to be afraid
tener sed	teh-nehr sehd	v to be thirsty
tener sueño	teh-nehr soo-eh-nyoh	v to be sleepy
la terminal	lah tehr-mee-nahl	terminal (f)
terminar	tehr-mee-nahr	v to finish
término medio	tehr-mee-noh meh-dee-oh	medium
la ternera	lah tehr-neh-rah	veal
la tía	lah tee-ah	aunt
la tienda de abarrotes	lah-tyehn-dah deh ah-bah-rroh-tehs	grocery store (f)
la tienda de departamentos	lah tyehn-dah deh deh-par-tah-mehn-tohs	department store
la tienda de perfumes	lah tyehn-dah deh pehr-foo-mehss	perfume store
el tío	ehl tee-oh	uncle (m)
la toalla	lah toh-ah-yah	towel
todos	toh-doh ehl moon-doh	everyone
tomar	toh-mahr	v to take
la torta	lah tohr-tah	cake
la tos	lah tohss	n cough
toser	toh-sehr	v to cough
trabajar	trah-bah-khahr	v to work
el transporte público	ehl trahns-pohr-teh poo-blee-koh	public transportation (m)
el tren	ehl trehn	train
tres cuartos	trehs kwahr-tohs	medium rare
tú	too	you (sing. inf.)

adj adjective   v verb   adv adverb   n noun

U

usted/ustedes	oo-stehd/oo-stehd-ehss	you (sing./pl. form.)

V

las vacaciones	lahs bah-kah-syohn-ehs	vacation (f pl.)
validar (validación)	bah-lee-dahr (bah-lee-dah-syohn)	v to accept, to validate
el vaso	ehl bah-sso	glass
vegetariano puro/ vegetariana pura	beh-kheh-tah-ryah-noh poo-roh/beh-kheh-tah-ryah-nah poo-rah	vegan (m/f)
vegetariano/ vegetariana	beh-kheh-tah-ryah-noh/ beh-kheh-tah-ryah-nah	vegetarian (m/f)
la venda	lah behn-dah	bandage [plaster]
vender	behn-dehr	v to sell
venir	beh-neer	v to come
ver	behr	v to see
verdadero	behr-dah-deh-roh	true, real
verde	behr-deh	green
vestirse	behs-teer-seh	v to get dressed
viajar	byah-khahr	to travel
el viaje de negocios	ehl byah-kheh deh neh-goh-syohs	business trip
la vieira	lah vyeh-ee-rah	scallop
viejo/vieja	byeh-khoh/byeh-khah	old (m/f)
el vino blanco/rojo	ehl bee-noh blahn-koh/rroh-khoh	white/red wine
la visa	lah bee-sah	visa
visitar	bee-see-tahr	v to visit
voltear	bohl-teh-ahr	v to turn
volver	bohl-behr	v to return
vomitar	boh-mee-tahr	v to throw up
el vuelo	ehl bweh-loh	flight

W

le WiFi	ehl wee-fee	WiFi

Y

yo	yoh	I

Days

el lunes	ehl loo-nehs	Monday
el martes	ehl mahr-tehs	Tuesday
el miércoles	ehl myehr-koh-lehs	Wednesday
el jueves	ehl khweh-behs	Thursday
el viernes	ehl byehr-nehs	Friday
el sábado	ehl sah-bah-doh	Saturday
el domingo	ehl doh-meen-goh	Sunday

Months

enero	eh-neh-roh	January
febrero	feh-breh-roh	February
marzo	mahr-soh	March
abril	ah-breel	April
mayo	mah-yoh	May
junio	khoo nyoh	June
julio	khoo-lyoh	July
agosto	ah-gohs-toh	August
septiembre	sehp-tyehm-breh	September
octubre	ohk-too-breh	October
noviembre	noh-byehm-breh	November
diciembre	dee-syehm-breh	December

Countries/Nationalities

	Alemania	ah-leh-mah-nyah	Germany
	alemán	ah-leh-mahn	German m
	alemana	ah-leh-mah-nah	German f
	Australia	awh-strah-lyah	Australia
	australiano	awh-strah-lyah-no	Australian m
	australiana	awh-strah-lyah-nah	Australian f
	Canadá	kah-nah-dah	Canada
	canadiense	kah-nah-dyen-seh	Canadian
	España	eh-spah-nyah	Spain
	español	ehs-pah-nyohl	Spanish m
	española	ehs-pah-nyoh-lah	Spanish f
	los Estados Unidos	lohs ehs-tah-dohs oo-nee-dohs	United States
	estadounidense	eh-stah-doh-oo-nee-dehn-seh	American
	Francia	frahn-syah	France
	francés	frahn-sehs	French m
	francesa	frahn-seh-sah	French f
	Irlanda	eer-lahn-dah	Ireland
	irlandés	eer-lahn-dehs	Irish m
	irlandesa	eer-lahn-deh-sah	Irish f
	Italia	ee-tah-lyah	Italy
	italiano	ee-tah-lyah-noh	Italian m
	italiana	ee-tah-lyah-nah	Italian f
	México	meh-khee-koh	Mexico
	mexicano	meh-khee-kah-noh	Mexican m
	mexicana	meh-khee-kah-nah	Mexican f

adj	adjective		v	verb	adv	adverb	n noun

Perú	peh-<u>roo</u>	Peru
peruano	peh-roo-<u>ah</u>-noh	Peruvian m
peruana	peh-roo-<u>ah</u>-nah	Peruvian f
Portugal	pohr-too-<u>gahl</u>	Portugal
portugués	pohr-too-<u>ghehs</u>	Portuguese m
portuguesa	pohr-too-<u>gheh</u>-sah	Portuguese f
el Reino Unido	ehl <u>reyee</u>-noh oo-<u>nee</u>-doh	United Kingdom
inglés	een-<u>glehs</u>	English m
inglesa	een-<u>gleh</u>-sah	English f

Colors

amarillo ah-mah-<u>reeyoh</u> yellow	negro neh-groh black
azul ah-<u>sool</u> blue	rojo <u>roh</u>-khoh red
blanco <u>blahn</u>-koh white	rosa <u>roh</u>-sah rose
morado moh-<u>rah</u>-doh purple	verde <u>behr</u>-deh green

Numbers

uno	<u>oo</u>-noh	1
dos	dohs	2
tres	trehs	3
cuatro	<u>kwah</u>-troh	4
cinco	<u>seen</u>-koh	5
seis	seyees	6
siete	<u>seeyeh</u>-teh	7
ocho	<u>oh</u>-choh	8
nueve	<u>nweh</u>-beh	9
diez	deeyehs	10
once	<u>ohn</u>-seh	11
doce	<u>doh</u>-seh	12
trece	<u>treh</u>-seh	13
catorce	kah-<u>tohr</u>-seh	14
quince	<u>keen</u>-seh	15
dieciséis	dyeh-see-<u>seyees</u>	16
diecisiete	dyeh-see-<u>seeyeh</u>-teh	17
dieciocho	dyeh-see-<u>oh</u>-choh	18
diecinueve	dyeh-see-<u>nweh</u>-beh	19
veinte	<u>beh-een</u>-teh	20
treinta	<u>treh-een</u>-tah	30
treinta y uno	<u>treh-een</u>-tah ee <u>oo</u>-noh	31
treinta y dos	<u>treh-een</u>-tah ee dohs	32
treinta y tres	<u>treh-een</u>-tah ee trehs	33
treinta y cuatro	<u>treh-een</u>-tah ee <u>kwah</u>-troh	34
treinta y cinco	<u>treh-een</u>-tah ee <u>seen</u>-koh	35
cuarenta	kwah-<u>rehn</u>-tah	40
cincuenta	seen-<u>kwehn</u>-tah	50
sesenta	seh-<u>sehn</u>-tah	60
setenta	seh-<u>tehn</u>-tah	70
ochenta	oh-<u>chehn</u>-tah	80
noventa	noh-<u>behn</u>-tah	90
cien	syehn	100

Clothing Sizes

Women's Dresses			Men's Dress Shirts		
USA	UK	Spain	USA	UK	Spain
4	6	34	14	14	35
6	8	36	14½	14½	37
8	10	38	15	15	38
10	12	40	15½	15½	39
12	14	42	16	16	41
14	16	44	16½	16½	42
16	18	46	17	17	44

Women's Shoes			Men's Shoes		
USA	UK	Spain	USA	UK	Spain
5	2½	34½	6	5½	22
6	3½	36	7	6½	23
7	4½	38	8	7½	24
8	5½	39	9	8½	25
9	6½	40	10	9½	26½
10	7½	41½	11	10½	27½
12	9½	44	12	11½	29

adj adjective	v verb	adv adverb	n noun

Unit 1 Lesson 1

Activity A 1 F; 2 T; 3 F; 4 T

Activity B

¿Adónde va usted de vacaciones?; Yo voy a Barcelona.; ¿Va usted en avión?; No, voy a tomar el tren.

Lesson 2

Activity A 1 c; 2 a; 3 d; 4 b; 5 e

Activity B

1 el avión; 2 el bote; 3 la limosina; 4 el coche; 5 la bici

Lesson 3

Activity A 1 crucero; 2 taxis; 3 coche; 4 avión

Activity B

1 ¿En dónde se encuentra la parada de taxis?; 2 Voy a alquilar un coche.; 3 Ella está tomando un bote.; 4 ¿Hay servicio de limosina?

Lesson 4

Activity A 1 Yo; 2 Él; 3 Ella; 4 Ustedes

Activity B 1 Nosotros; 2 Ellas; 3 Vosotros; 4 Ellos

Lesson 5

Activity A

1 boleto; 2 maletas; 3 dólares/libras esterlinas, euros; 4 pasaporte; 5 coche

Activity B

Answers may vary. Possible answers:
1 comprar un boleto; 2 hacer mis maletas; 3 encontrar un hotel; 4 reservar un coche de alquiler; 5 aprender un poco de español.

Lesson 6

Activity A

1 martes; 2 viernes; 3 lunes; 4 sábado; 5 miércoles; 6 domingo; 7 jueves

Activity B

1 enero; 2 febrero; 3 marzo; 4 abril; 5 mayo; 6 junio; 7 julio; 8 agosto; 9 septiembre; 10 octubre; 11 noviembre; 12 diciembre

Lesson 7

Activity A

1 registrarse en línea; 2 número de reservación; 3 imprimir el boleto de embarque

Activity B 1 b; 2 d; 3 c; 4 a

Activity C

1 Click on registrarse en línea.; 2 Enter your número de reservación.; 3 Click on elegir su asiento.; 4 Click on imprimir la tarjeta de embarque.

Activity D

1 Click on modificar el día y la hora del vuelo.; 2 Click on Elegir su asiento.; 3 Click on Los horarios de vuelo actualizados

Lesson 8

Activity A

1 vamos; 2 va; 3 voy; 4 van; 5 vais; 6 vas; 7 va; 8 van

Activity B

1 Sí, nosotros vamos a Barcelona.; 2 Sí, vosotros vais a Galicia.; 3 Sí, ellos van a Venezuela. 4 Sí, yo voy a Mallorca.

Activity C 1 vamos; 2 va; 3 voy; 4 van; 5 vas

Review

Activity A 1 el tren; 2 el avión; 3 la limosina; 4 el coche

Activity B

Marc   ¿Adónde va de vacaciones?
Christine   Yo voy a Barcelona.
Marc   ¿Va usted en avión?
Christine   No, yo voy a tomar el tren.

Activity C

1 lunes; 2 martes; 3 miércoles; 4 jueves; 5 viernes; 6 sábado; 7 domingo

Activity D

yo	voy
tú	vas
él/ella	va
nosotros	vamos
vosotros	vais
ellos/ellas	van

Activity E

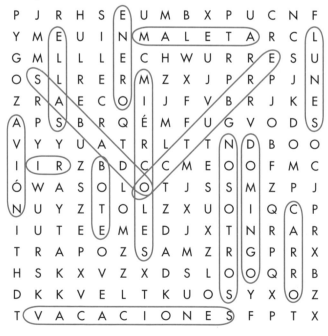

Unit 2 Lesson 1

Activity A

1 T; 2 T; 3 F; 4 F

Activity B

Yo me llamo (your name).; Sí, yo soy americano/americana./No, yo no soy americano/americana.; Sí, yo estoy de vacaciones./No, yo no estoy de vacaciones.

Lesson 2

Activity A

1 tres; 2 dos; 3 cuatro; 4 cinco

Activity B

1 14h40; 2 14h05; 3 14h30; 4 13h55

Activity C

1 06.62.68.10.08
2 01.45.54.16.17
3 04.13.22.14.31

Lesson 3

Activity A

1 Yo estoy bien, gracias.; 2 Yo me llamo (your name).; 3 Yo soy de (where you're from).

Activity B

1 ¡Hola!; 2 Buenos días.; 3 Buenas tardes.; 4 Buenas noches.

Lesson 4

Activity A

1 es; 2 son; 3 somos; 4 están

Activity B

1 Sí, yo estoy de vacaciones./Sí, nosotros estamos de vacaciones.; 2 Sí, Jerónimo es español.; 3 Sí, Catalina y Julia son americanas.; 4 Sí, ellos están en el tren.; 5 Sí, yo estoy en el bus.

Activity C

yo	soy	nosotros/nosotras	somos
tú	eres	vosotros/vosotras	sois
usted	es	ustedes	son
él/ella	es	ellos/ellas	son

Your Turn

Answers may vary. Possible answers: joven, rubio/rubia, guapo/guapa, español/española, americano/americana

Lesson 5

Activity A

1 El próximo tren es a las 19h30.; 2 El próximo tren es a las 19h35.; 3 El próximo tren es a las 19h50.

Activity B

1 Bilbao; 2 Sevilla; 3 Barcelona; 4 Málaga

Lesson 6

Activity A 1 e; 2 d; 3 a; 4 c; 5 f; 6 b

Activity B 1 el español; 2 el alemán; 3 el inglés; 4 el italiano

Activity C

1 d; 2 a; 3 c; 4 b

Lesson 7

Activity A

Answers will vary.

Activity B

1 Ellos van a esquiar.; 2 Ella está en viaje de negocios.; 3 Ellos van a hacer montañismo.; 4 Él va a aprender español en Madrid.; 5 Ellos están de vacaciones.

Lesson 8

Activity A

1 la estación; 2 el bote; 3 la pregunta; 4 el peaje

Activity B

1 f; 2 m; 3 f; 4 m; 5 f

Review

Activity A

sesenta y dos; once; diecinueve

Activity B

1 Yo soy estadounidense y hablo inglés.; 2 Yo soy francesa y hablo francés.; 3 Yo soy inglés y hablo inglés.

Activity C

1 noventa y uno, tres cuarenta y cinco, treinta y dos, veintiuno; 2 noventa y uno, siete diecinueve, catorce sesenta y tres; 3 noventa y uno, siete cuarenta y nueve, veintiuno, cincuenta y ocho

Activity D

1 18h05; 2 3h15; 3 12h30; 4 6h45

Activity E

1 la; 2 la; 3 la; 4 las; 5 el

Challenge

Answers may vary. Possible answers: 1 Francia, francés/francesa, el francés; 2 Los Estados Unidos, estadounidense, el inglés; 3 Inglaterra, inglés/inglesa, el inglés; 4 Italia, italiano/italiana, el italiano; 5 España, español/española, el español

Unit 3 Lesson 1

Activity A

Apellido: Smith; Nombre: Margaret; Nacionalidad: Estadounidense; Fecha de nacimiento: 05 de marzo de 1975; Fecha del vuelo: 23 de marzo de 2010; Número del vuelo: 2083

Activity B

1 b; 2 d; 3 a; 4 e; 5 c

Lesson 2

Activity A

1 a; 2 e; 3 b; 4 c; 5 d

Activity B

1 llegar a la terminal; 2 pasar el control de pasaportes; 3 llegar al retiro de equipaje; 4 pasar la aduana; 5 buscar la salida

Activity C

Lesson 3

Activity A

1 b; 2 a; 3 a; 4 b

Activity B

1 este; 2 estos; 3 esta; 4 estos

Lesson 4

Activity A

1 tenemos; 2 tengo; 3 tiene; 4 tienen

Activity B

1 c; 2 b; 3 e; 4 a; 5 d

Lesson 5

Activity A

1 F; 2 T; 3 F; 4 T

Activity B

Nosotros vamos al hotel El Prado.; Prado 11. ¿Puedo pagarle con tarjeta de crédito?; ¿Me puede dar un recibo por favor ?

Activity C

1 ¿Cuál es la dirección?; 2 Lo siento.; 3 Sólo puede pagar en efectivo.

Lesson 6

Activity A

1 a; 2 b; 3 b

Activity B

1 Elija "comprar billetes."; 2 Elija "billete sencillo."; 3 Validar.; 4 Pagar.

Lesson 7

Activity A

Casa de Campo

Activity B

1 Ópera; 2 Callao

Lesson 8

Activity A

1 la; 2 el; 3 el

Activity B

1 una; 2 un; 3 unos

Activity C

1 las; 2 el; 3 la; 4 unos/unas

Review

Activity A

Apellido (your last name); Nombre (your first name); Nacionalidad (your nationality); Fecha de nacimiento (your birth date); Lugar de nacimiento (your place of birth)

Activity B

1 ¿Me puede dar un recibo por favor?; 2 ¿Puedo pagarle con tarjeta de crédito?; 3 ¿Cuál es la dirección?

Challenge

Answers may vary. Possible answers:; 1 Yo tengo hambre.; 2 Yo tengo sed.; 3 Yo tengo sueño.; 4 Yo tengo calor.; 5 Yo tengo miedo.

Activity C

1 una maleta; 2 un bote; 3 unos carros

Activity D

1 En Sol tome la línea 3 hasta Callao. En Callao cambie a la línea 5 hacia Núñez de Balboa y siga dos estaciones. Baje en Chueca.
2 Suba en Callao, tome la línea 5 hacia Casa de Campo. En la siguiente estación tome la línea R. Continúe hasta la última estación.

Unit 4 Lesson 1

Activity A 1 siete noches; 2 dos personas; 3 sesenta y cinco

Activity B 1 hotel; 2 reserva; 3 personas; 4 euros

Activity C

1 Buenos días. Tengo una reserva a nombre de (your name).;
2. ¿Cuánto es por noche?

Lesson 2

Activity A 1 F; 2 F; 3 T; 4 T; 5 F

Activity B 1 c; 2 d; 3 a; 4 b

Lesson 3

Activity A

1 Necesito una cama adicional.; 2 Hice una reserva por Internet.;
3 ¿Tiene usted una habitación para no fumador? ¿Tiene usted una
habitación para dos personas con baño?

Activity B

1 ¿Cuánto es por noche?; 2 ¿Tiene una habitación no fumador?;
3 ¿Tiene una habitación con aire acondicionado?; 4 ¿Tiene una
habitación para dos personas?

Lesson 4

Activity A

1 La habitación no está en la planta baja.; 2 No hay cuarto de baño
en la habitación.; 3 La ducha no funciona.; 4 No necesito una cuna.

Activity B

1 Harry no es francés.; 2 El teléfono no funciona.; 3 No hay una
bañera.; 4 Peter no habla español.

Lesson 5

Activity A

1 No, es grande.; 2 Sí, hay una televisión; 3 Sí, hay un escritorio
y una silla.

Activity B

1 mi; 2 su; 3 su; 4 sus

Lesson 6

Activity A la escalera

Activity B 1 toallas; 2 papel higiénico; 3 champú; 4 jabón

Activity C

Answers may vary. Possible answers:
la habitación: la manta, la sábana, la almohada, la cafetera
el cuarto de baño: el lavabo, el jabón, la toalla, el champú

Lesson 7

Activity A

1 ¿Me podría despertar a las siete?; 2 ¿Me podría llamar un taxi ?;
3 ¿A qué hora debo desocupar la habitación?; 4 ¿Podría arreglar
la habitación?

Activity B 1 b; 2 a; 3 d; 4 c

Activity C 1 b; 2 a; 3 d; 4 a

Lesson 8

Activity A

yo	hablo	nosotros/nosotras	hablamos
tú	hablas	vosotros/vosotras	habláis
usted	habla	ustedes	hablan
él/ella	habla	ellos/ellas	hablan

Activity B 1 hablan; 2 visitamos; 3 estudio; 4 paga; 5 busca

Activity C 1 c; 2 e; 3 a; 4 b; 5 d

Review

Activity A

1 la cama; 2 la secadora de pelo; 3 las toallas; 4 la ducha

Activity B

1 Usted no estudia español.
2 La plancha no funciona.
3 Nosotros no visitamos el Palacio Real.
4 Las habitaciones no son pequeñas.

Activity C

1 mi teléfono; 2 su habitaciónn; 3 sus mantas; 4 su llave

Activity D

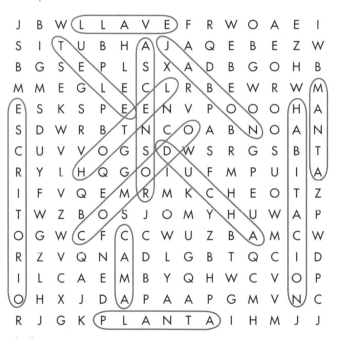

Challenge

yo pregunto; tú preguntas; usted pregunta; él/ella pregunta;
nosotros preguntamos; vosotros/vosotras preguntáis; ustedes
preguntan; ellos/ellas preguntan
yo bailo; tú bailas; usted baila; él/ella baila; nosotros/nosotras
bailamos; vosotros/vosotras bailáis; ustedes bailan; ellos/ellas bailan
yo trabajo; tú trabajas; usted trabaja; él/ella trabaja; nosotros/
nosotras trabajamos; vosotros/vosotras trabajáis; ustedes trabajan; ellos/ellas trabajan
yo amo; tú amas; usted ama; él/ella ama; nosotros/nosotras amamos; vosotros/vosotras amáis; ustedes aman; ellos/ellas aman

Answer Key

Unit 5 Lesson 1

Activity A 1 T; 2 F; 3 F; 4 T

Activity B

Ana	¿Qué vamos a hacer hoy?
Felipe	Yo tengo que ir al banco.
Ana	¿Podemos visitar el Palacio Real?
Felipe	¡Sí! Yo quisiera visitar una iglesia también.
Ana	¡Tenemos muchas cosas para hacer!

Lesson 2

Activity A 1 la iglesia; 2 el correo; 3 el banco; 4 el castillo

Activity B

1 la oficina de turismo; 2 el mercado; 3 el parque; 4 el museo

Activity C 1 d; 2 c; 3 a; 4 b; 5 f; 6 e

Your Turn

Answers may vary. Possible answers:
1 el castillo; 2 el monumento; 3 el museo; 4 el parque

Lesson 3

Activity A 1 dólares/euros; 2 libras/dólares; 3 euros/libras

Activity B

1 La tasa de cambio es 1 euro por un dólar cuarenta.; 2 El banco cierra a las 4:30.; 3 El banco abre a las 9:00.; 4 Hay un cajero automático en el banco.

Activity C

1 El cajero automático se comió mi tarjeta.; 2 ¿A qué hora abre el banco?; 3 Yo quiero cambiar cheques de viajero por euros.; 4 ¿Dónde está el cajero automático más cercano?; 5 ¿Cuál es la tasa de cambio?; 6 ¿A qué hora cierra el banco?

Your Turn

Answers may vary. Possible answers:
Yo quiero cambiar unos dólares por euros.; Yo quiero cambiar unas libras por euros.

Lesson 4

Activity A

yo	veo	yo	puedo
tú	ves	tú	puedes
usted	ve	usted	puede
él/ella	ve	él/ella	puede
nosotros/nosotras	vemos	nosotros/nosotras	podemos
vosotros/vosotras	veis	vosotros/vosotras	podéis
ustedes	ven	ustedes	pueden
ellos/ellas	ven	ellos/ellas	pueden

Activity B

Ana	¡Yo veo la Plaza de la Armería!
Felipe	¿En dónde? Yo no puedo verla!
Ana	¿Tú ves el Palacio Real?
Felipe	¡Sí, Nosotros vemos varios edificios!

Activity C

1 Sí, nosotros podemos ir de vacaciones.; 2 Sí, nosotros vemos el museo.; 3 Sí, nosotros podemos visitar el castillo.; 4 Sí, nosotros vemos el cajero automático.; 5 Sí, la oficina de cambio de divisas puede cambiar dólares a euros.; 6 Sí, ellos ven el municipio.

Lesson 5

Activity A

1 Vaya a la izquierda.; 2 Continúe recto.; 3 Vaya a la derecha.; 4 Tome la segunda calle a la izquierda.

Activity B 1 Palacio Real de El Pardo; 2 Museo del Prado

Lesson 6

Activity A

1 dieciocho centavos; 2 tres euros con setenta centavos; 3 treinta y cinco euros; 4 veinte euros

Activity B

1 mil quinientos euros con sesenta centavos; 2 noventa y nueve euros con noventa y nueve centavos; 3 setenta y cinco centavos

Lesson 7

Activity A 1 c; 2 b; 3 a; 4 d

Activity B

1 ¿Puede usted repetirlo?; 2 ¿Qué quiere decir eso?; 3 Estoy perdido/perdida.; 4 Lo siento, no entiendo.; 5 ¿Puede usted mostrarme en el mapa?; 6 Yo busco el banco.; 7 ¿Puede usted hablar más lentamente?; 8 ¿Puede usted indicarme el camino?

Lesson 8

Activity A 1 cuándo; 2 quién; 3 cuánto; 4 dónde

Activity B 1 Cuánto; 2 Cómo; 3 Dónde; 4 Quién

Activity C 1 e; 2 d; 3 f; 4 b; 5 c; 6 a

Activity D

Crossword:
1 (down) C
2 (across) QUIEN
3 (down) Q
4 (across) CUANTO
down: CUANDO, QANDE
5 (across) DONDE

Review

Activity A 1 el puente; 2 el museo; 3 la iglesia; 4 el castillo

Activity B 1 podemos; 2 podéis; 3 puedo; 4 pueden

Activity C

yo	veo	nosotros/nosotras	vemos
tú	ves	vosotros/vosotras	veis
usted	ve	ustedes	ven
él/ella	ve	ellos/ellas	ven

Activity D

1 ¿Puede usted hablar más lentamente?; 2 ¿Puede usted escribirlo?; 3 ¿Cuánto es?; 4 ¿Dónde está la iglesia?

Activity E 1 d; 2 a; 3 g; 4 b; 5 f; 6 e; 7 c

Challenge

1 seiscientos noventa y dos; 2 mil trescientos noventa y nueve; 3 dos mil diez; 4 setenta y siete

Answer Key

Unit 6 Lesson 1

Activity A 1 un restaurante; 2 española/francesa; 3 tapería; 4 frente a

Activity B 1 No, a él le gusta la comida española y francesa.; 2 Sí, hay una buena tapería al lado del correo.; 3 No, la tapería no está lejos del correo.; 4 El correo está frente a la iglesia.

Activity C 1 c; 2 b; 3 e; 4 f; 5 a; 6 d

Lesson 2

Activity A 1 la torta; 2 el queso; 3 el pan; 4 la ensalada; 5 el filete

Activity B Answers will vary.

Lesson 3

Activity A 1 el tenedor; 2 la cuchara; 3 el cuchillo; 4 el vaso

Activity B 1 un vaso; 2 un tenedor; 3 una servilleta

Activity C 1 Yo soy vegetariano/vegetariana.; 2 ¿Me puede traer la cuenta por favor?; 3 Yo soy alérgico a los camarones.; 4 Yo voy a pedir la ensalada.

Your Turn

Answers will vary. Possible answers:
Yo voy a pedir la ensalada como entrada.; Yo voy a pedir el pollo.; Yo voy a pedir un vaso de vino rojo.

Lesson 4

Activity A 1 van a pedir; 2 vas a pedir; 3 voy a pedir; 4 vamos a pedir; 5 van a pedir

Activity B 1 Juan va a pedir la ensalada.; 2 Nosotros vamos a pedir la sopa.; 3 Vosotros vais a pedir los camarones.

Activity C 1 Un vegetariano puede pedir la ensalada.; 2 Para comer la ensalada pido un tenedor.; 3 En España pedimos primero la entrada, después el plato principal.; 4 No, pedimos el desayuno por la mañana.

Lesson 5

Activity A Cristina: a, b, d, e; Martín: c, e

Activity B 1 Yo voy a pedir el almuerzo.; 2 Yo voy a pedir el flan como postre.; 3 Yo voy a pedir el filete, bien cocido.; 4 Yo voy a pedir una botella de vino.

Lesson 6

Activity A 1 Jean pide una coca.; 2 Kathy y Michelle piden un café.; 3 Nosotros pedimos una botella de vino rojo.; 4 Yo pido una cerveza.

Activity B

Activity C

Answers may vary. Possible answers:
el desayuno: el café, el té, el jugo de naranja
el almuerzo: el té helado, la coca cola, el agua
la cena: el vino blanco, el vino rojo, la cerveza, el agua

Activity D 1 b; 2 f; 3 a; 4 e; 5 d; 6 c

Lesson 7

Activity A

1 ¿Qué le puedo servir?; 2 ¡Buen provecho!; 3 ¿Ha terminado?; 4 ¿Estuvo bien todo?

Activity B

1 agua; 2 un aperitivo; 3 agua mineral; 4 un digestivo

Activity C

Answer may vary. Possible answers:
Yo voy a pedir el almuerzo con el pollo, la ensalada y la torta de chocolate; Sí, todo estuvo bien.

Lesson 8

Activity A		Activity B	
yo	quiero	yo	bebo
tú	quieres	tú	bebes
usted	quiere	usted	bebe
él/ella	quiere	él/ella	bebe
nosotros/nosotras	queremos	nosotros/nosotras	bebemos
vosotros/vosotras	queréis	vosotros/vosotras	bebéis
ustedes	quieren	ustedes	beben
ellos/ellas	quieren	ellos/ellas	beben

Activity C 1 quiere; 2 quiero; 3 quieren; 4 queremos

Activity D 1 bebe; 2 bebéis; 3 bebes; 4 beben

Review

Activity A

1 ¿Puede traerme la cuenta, por favor?; 2 Yo voy a pedir el pollo.; 3 Yo voy a beber café.; 4 ¿Dónde está el baño?

Activity B 1 el pan; 2 el café; 3 la torta; 4 el jugo de naranja

Activity C 1 el cuchillo; 2 el mejillón; 3 un digestivo

Activity D

1 chocolate; 2 café; 3 cuchara; 4 tenedor; 5 pan
Bonus word: tarta

Activity E 1 quiere; 2 bebemos; 3 pedís; 4 quieren; 5 bebo; 6 pides

Challenge

yo pido; tú pides; usted pide; él/ella pide; nosotros/nosotras pedimos; vosotros/vosotras pedís; ellos/ellas piden
yo quiero; tú quieres; usted quiere; él/ella quiere; nosotros/nosotras queremos; vosotros/vosotras queréis; ustedes quieren; ellos/ellas quieren
yo bebo; tú bebes; usted bebe; él/ella bebe; nosotros/nosotras bebemos; vosotros/vosotras bebéis; ustedes beben; ellos/ellas beben

Unit 7 Lesson 1

Activity A

1 la Duquesa de Alba; 2 la camiseta de Madrid; 3 el libro España; 4 la taza

Activity B

1 no; 2 sí; 3 sí; 4 sí

Activity C

Answers may vary. Possible answers:
1 la camiseta Madrid; 2 la muñeca bailaora de flamenco; 3 el llavero flamenco; 4 el libro España

Lesson 2

Activity A

1 la tienda de chocolates; 2 la joyería; 3 la panadería; 4 la librería

Activity B

1 el centro comercial; 2 la tienda de chocolates; 3 la librería; 4 la perfumería

Activity C

1 b; 2 d; 3 e; 4 a; 5 c

Lesson 3

Activity A

1 d; 2 a; 3 b; 4 c

Activity B

1 ¿Es su mejor precio?; 2 Tengo que pensarlo. 3 Sólo estoy mirando.; 4 Sólo tengo 20 euros.

Lesson 4

Activity A

yo vendo; tú vendes; usted vende; él/ella vende; nosotros/nosotras vendemos; vosotros/vosotras vendéis; ustedes venden; ellos/ellas venden

Activity B

yo termino; tú terminas; usted termina; él/ella termina; nosotros/nosotras terminamos; vosotros/vosotras termináis; ustedes terminan; ellos/ellas terminan

Activity C

1 espera; 2 respondemos; 3 terminamos; 4 engordan

Lesson 5

Activity A

a (el cinturón, el bolso, la corbata)

Activity B

Answers may vary. Possible answers:
1 el pantalón, la camisa, el cinturón; 2 la camisa, la corbata, el abrigo; 3 la chaqueta, el cinturón, la corbata

Activity C

204€

Activity D

```
V F I Z K K F D R R M N P Q V B C W Y T Z G T C V S N T P A
U Q B T T N N F X V O P L I J N B H O T M D Q O U T L Q L F
W C Y D D G Y G U R T H V I K T M S A Q C Q B R L K T P L U
N V L A J A Y S U F X Z Q P R K I R B Q G V D B Y H Y N Y Z
H Q J O C P N T O B H B G E J T U I C I U B S A P W H T O B
P C U C Z Z N G J H X M Z R G A Y J O C A E L T S U Q X R D
C F D W Y I W S W W G F O M W I T P P G P O T A O Y Y F T L
R O H I C U D W Q Z N I Y J T N Q P Q P N Y S A D S A U C O
M Q L E W Y L W D M Z Y A R G Y U D Q W K N T T R O V B A G
J P H N E T J P I S R K Q L J S Y H Z X R A J H O Z R B Q X
A S I M A C C H D P R U J Z P Z G H C U H E D O X N R V O V
I T Y N X J K L J O J E N E J X J Q D G R J X Y S I F B O E
K B C E S R V F X D O B T S S H G Y X F E F K C G L S H C F
S L S S S L Z E P G O X I M R E Y P L T X Y D O V L O F X A
M F Q U Q V B W I D H G N X E D I I P A N T A L Ó N N B J C
```

Lesson 6

Activity A 1 una joya; 2 juguete; 3 productos de belleza; 4 tarjeta postal

Activity B 2; 3; 1

Activity C 1 c; 2 d; 3 a; 4 b

Activity D Answers may vary. Possible answers:
una joya; una caja de chocolates; una botella de vino; los productos de belleza; la ropa

Lesson 7

Activity A 1 c; 2 a; 3 b

Activity B 1 b; 2 b; 3 a

Lesson 8

Activity A 1 bonito; 2 caros; 3 pequeña; 4 fea

Activity B 1 un suéter verde; 2 un pantalón negro; 3 una camisa gris; 4 un cinturón azul

Review

Activity A 1 el supermercado; 2 el centro comercial; 3 la tienda de ropa; 4 la licorería

Activity B 1 ¿Cuánto cuesta?; 2 ¿Es verdadero?; 3 ¿Me puede dar un descuento?; 4 ¿En dónde está la caja?

Challenge

1 yo como; tú comes; usted come; él/ella come; nosotros/nosotras comemos; vosotros/vosotras coméis; ustedes comen; ellos/ellas comen
2 yo compro; tú compras; usted compra; él/ella compra; nosotros/nosotras compramos; vosotros/vosotras compráis; ustedes compran; ellos/ellas compran
3 yo escucho; tú escuchas; usted escucha; él/ella escucha; nosotros/nosotras escuchamos; vosotros/vosotras escucháis; ustedes escuchan; ellos/ellas escuchan

Activity C 1 b; 2 b; 3 a; 4 a

Activity D

Drawings will vary.
1 a small black car; 2 a large bottle of red wine; 3 a beautiful blue pair of jeans

Unit 8 Lesson 1

Activity A
1 b; 2 b; 3 a

Activity B

Robert	¿Hay un cibercafé cerca del hotel? Yo quiero leer mi correo electrónico.
Concierge	Sí. Hay un cibercafé al frente.
Robert	¿Tienen servicio de WiFi? Yo tengo mi ordenador portátil.
Concierge	Hay WiFi gratuito en el café al final de la calle.
Robert	¡Perfecto! Muchas gracias.

Activity C
1 Él quiere leer su correo electrónico.; 2 Hay un cibercafé frente al hotel.; 3 Hay WiFi gratuito en el café al final de la calle.

Lesson 2

Activity A
1 a; 2 b; 3 a

Activity B
1 el ratón; 2 la impresora; 3 la pantalla; 4 el teclado; 5 el Internet

Activity C
1 el celular; 2 el ordenador portátil; 3 el adaptador; 4 la memoria de USB

Lesson 3

Activity A
1 ¿Hay puntos de WiFi gratuitos?; 2 ¿Cuánto cuestan diez minutos de acceso?; 3 Yo necesito mandar un correo electrónico.; 4 ¿Dónde puedo comprar un paquete prepago de Internet?

Activity B
1 ¿Cuánto cuestan 30 minutos de acceso?; 2 ¿Hay WiFi en este hotel?; 3 ¿Puedo imprimir mi boleto de embarque?; 4 ¿Hay puntos de WiFi gratuitos?

Lesson 4

Activity A
1 hace; 2 haces; 3 hacéis; 4 hace; 5 hago; 6 hacen

Activity B
1 a; 2 b; 3 a; 4 b

Activity C
1 Hace buen día.; 2 Hace frío.; 3 Hace calor.; 4 Hace mal tiempo.

Lesson 5

Activity A
1 F; 2 T; 3 F; 4 T

Activity B
1 Levante el auricular; 2 Introduzca la tarjeta o marque el número gratuito; 3 Marque el número; 4 Cuelgue; 5 Retire su tarjeta

Activity C
1 a; 2 b; 3 b; 4 b

Lesson 6

Activity A 1 hacer click; 2 escribir; 3 imprimir; 4 prender

Activity B

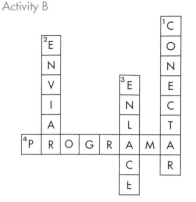

Activity C 1 a; 2 a; 3 b; 4 a

Lesson 7

Activity A 1 c; 2 a; 3 b

Activity B Es Ramón.; ¿Puedo hablar con Anna?

Activity C 1 Es(your name).; 2 Ha marcado el número equivocado.; 3 ¿Aló?; 4 Dígale que me llame, por favor.

Lesson 8

Activity A yo escribo; tú lees; ella dice; nosotros escribimos; ustedes leen; ellos dicen

Activity B 1 Sí, yo escribo a mis amigos.; 2 Sí, yo leo mi correo con frecuencia..; 3 Yo digo aló?".

Activity C 1. Martín lee.; 2. Manuela escribe.; 3 Vicente dice ¡Buenos días!"

Review

Activity A
1 ¿Hay un cibercafé cerca del hotel ?; 2 ¿Dónde puedo comprar un paquete prepagado de Internet?; 3 ¿Puedo imprimir mi boleto de embarque?; 4 ¿Puedo hablar con (name)?

Activity B

yo	escribo	leo
tú	escribes	lees
usted	escribe	lee
él/ella	escribe	lee
nosotros/nosotras	escribimos	leemos
vosotros/vosotras	escribís	leéis
ustedes	escriben	leen
ellos/ellas	escriben	leen

Activity C 1 d; 2 a; 3 b; 4 e; 5 c; 6 g; 7 f

Activity D
1 Ellos caminan.; 2 Ella tiene calor.; 3. Nosotros hacemos fila.; 4 Yo hago mis maletas.

Challenge

Answers will vary. Possible answer:
A: ¿Aló?
B: Buenos días, es Marta. ¿Puedo hablar con Jim?
A: Jim no está. ¿Quiere dejar un mensaje?
B: Dígale que me llame, por favor.

Unit 9 Lesson 1

Activity A

1 Natalia quiere salir.; 2 Ella quiere ir a bailar.

Activity B

¡Yo quiero salir!; Yo quiero bailar. ¿Podemos ir a un club nocturno?; Sí, pero yo no puedo quedarme hasta muy tarde.

Lesson 2

Activity A 1 a; 2 b; 3 a; 4 b

Activity B

Answers may vary. Possible answers:
1 el café; 2 el cine; 3 el concierto

Activity C 1 al teatro; 2 al concierto de rock; 3 al cine; 4 al club nocturno; 5 al casino

Activity D 1 el casino; 2 el cine; 3 el café; 4 el club nocturno

Lesson 3

Activity A

1 Reinaldo ama la música clásica.; 2 Carlota y Martín aman la música española.; 3 Nosotros amamos el jazz.

Activity B 1 tiempo; 2 cuánto; 3 recomendar

Activity C

¿Cuánto cuesta el boleto?; ¿Cuánto tiempo dura?; ¿Cuándo termina el concierto?

Lesson 4

Activity A 1 a; 2 b; 3 b; 4 b

Activity B 1 al; 2 del; 3 a; 4 del

Activity C

Answers may vary. Possible answers:
1 Yo quiero ir al teatro.; 2 Yo quiero ir a la fiesta.; 3 Yo quiero ir al museo.

Activity D 1 al; 2 de la; 3 a; 4 al; 5 a los

Lesson 5

Activity A

1 Concierto de rock; 2 Calígula; 3 La Loba (Pop-Rock); Total: 25€

Activity B

Answers may vary. Possible answers:
1 Concierto de jazz; 2 Las cuatro estaciones de Vivaldi; 3 Carmina Burana

Activity C 1 a; 2 a; 3 a

Lesson 6

Activity A 1 la pista de baile; 2 el bar; 3 el guardarropa

Activity B 1 el guardia; 2 el disk jockey; 3 la barista

Activity C 1 b; 2 a; 3 a; 4 a; 5 a

Lesson 7

Activity A Answers may vary. Possible answers:
1 ¿Te puedo invitar una bebida?; 2 ¿Quieres bailar?; 3 ¿A qué te dedicas?

Activity B 1 ¿Hay alguien aquí?; 2 ¿Me puedo sentar con ustedes?; 3 ¿Les interrumpí?; 4 ¿Te puedo invitar una bebida?

Activity C 1 ¿Hay alguien aquí?; 2 ¿A qué se dedica?; 3 ¿Quiero bailar?; 4 ¿Me puedo sentar con usted?

Lesson 8

Activity A 1 decidimos; 2 deciden; 3 decido; 4 decide; 5 decides; 6 decide; 7 decide

Activity B 1 salen; 2 sale; 3 salís; 4 salir; 5 salgo; 6 salimos; 7 sale

Activity C Answers may vary. Possible answers:
1 Nosotros salimos tarde.; 2 Nosotros salimos al cine.; 3 Nosotros decidimos salir de vacaciones con nuestra familia.; 4 Nosotros salimos a Mallorca.

Activity D 1 a; 2 b; 3 a; 4 b

Review

Activity A Answers may vary. Possible answers:
1 el club nocturno; 2 el concierto; 3 el teatro

Activity B 1 a; 2 b; 3 b

Activity C

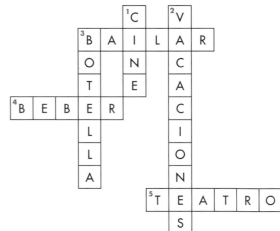

Activity D 1 a; 2 a; 3 b

Activity E

yo	salgo	decido
tú	sales	decides
usted	sale	decide
él/ella	sale	decide
nosotros/nosotras	salimos	decidimos
vosotros/vosotras	salís	decidís
ustedes	salen	deciden
ellos/ellas	salen	deciden

Answer Key

Unit 10 Lesson 1

Activity A

1 T; 2 T; 3 T; 4 T

Activity B

Busco una farmacia que esté abierta toda la noche.; ¿Podría usted indicarme el camino?; ¡Muchas gracias!

Lesson 2

Activity A

1 los bomberos (080); 2 la sala de urgencia (061); 3 la policía (092)

Activity B

1 el bombero; 2 el doctor; 3 la policía

Activity C 1 la farmacia; 2 la estación de policía; 3 el hospital

Lesson 3

Activity A

1 ¡Ladrón!; 2 ¡Fuego!; 3 ¡Socorro!; 4 ¡Cuidado!; 5 Me he roto la pierna.; 6 Yo soy diabético.

Activity B

1 Me he roto el brazo.; 2 Estoy enfermo.; 3 Me he roto la pierna.; 4 Yo soy asmático.

Activity C 1 socorro; 2 fuego; 3 cuidado; 4 ladrón

Activity D 1 c; 2 a; 3 d; 4 b

Lesson 4

Activity A 1 se; 2 nos; 3 te; 4 se

Activity B

1 Juana se cepilla los dientes.; 2 Anita se ducha.; 3 Él se llama Pablo.

Activity C 1 e; 2 a; 3 c; 4 b; 5 d

Lesson 5

Activity A

1 T; 2 T; 3 T; 4 F

Activity B

Me duele la cabeza.; Me siento enfermo.; Tengo la gripe.; Me duele la garganta.

Activity C

Él tose.; Le duele la cabeza.; Él tiene fiebre.

Your Turn

Answers may vary. Possible answers:
Yo me siento enfermo. Me duele la cabeza. Tengo tos y me duele la garganta. Creo que tengo la gripe.

Lesson 6

Activity A 1 el ojo; 2 la nariz; 3 la oreja; 4 la lengua

Activity B 1 el pie; 2 el brazo; 3 el pecho; 4 la mano

Activity C

Answers may vary. Possible answers:
el cuerpo: el brazo; la rodilla; el pie; la cabeza
la cara: la boca; la lengua; los ojos; la oreja; la nariz

Lesson 7

Activity A

las pastillas para la garganta; unas vendas; los antiácidos; la aspirina

Activity B

1 unas pastillas para la garganta; 2 una aspirina/un acetaminofén; 3 un jarabe para la tos

Activity C

1 ¿Qué me recomienda para la náusea?; 2 ¿Qué me recomienda para un catarro?; 3 ¿Qué me recomienda para el mareo?

Lesson 8

Activity A

comer	he comido
doemir	he dormido
vender	he vendido
beber	he bebido
contestar	he contestado
ver	he visto
escribir	he escrito
hacer	he hecho
pagar	he pagado

Activity B

Answers may vary. Possible answers:
1 Sí, yo he visitado el Museo Arqueológico Nacional./No, yo no he visitado el Museo Arqueológico Nacional.; 2 Sí, yo he pedido un postre./No, yo no he pedido un postre.; 3 Sí, yo he contestado el teléfono./No, yo no he contestado el teléfono.; 4 Sí, yo he comprado un vestido./No, yo no he comprado un vestido.; 5 Sí, yo he hecho mis maletas./No, yo no he hecho mis maletas.

Review

Activity A

1 Me han robado la billetera.; 2 ¡Socorro!; 3 Me he roto la pierna.; 4 Me duelen los pies.; 5 Me duele la garganta.

Activity B

1 Teófilo está enfermo.; 2 A Lucía le duele la espalda.; 3 Mateo se viste.; 4 Anita se cepilla los dientes.

Activity C

Me duele la cabeza; Tengo fiebre; Me duele la garganta; Tengo una tos fuerte

Activity D

1 Yo he viajado con mi familia.; 2 Nosotros hemos escogido el almuerzo.; 3 Ellas han comido una torta.; 4 Él ha contestado el teléfono.; 5 Tú has mirado la tele.

Challenge

Answers may vary. Possible answers:
el brazo, la cabeza, los ojos, la nariz, la pierna, el hombro, la oreja, la mano, el pie, la lengua

Answer Key

Unit 11 Lesson 1

Activity A 1 me divierto; 2 hecho; 3 visitado; 4 hablado; 5 comido

Activity B visitar el Museo de arte moderno; hablar con los españoles; comer mucho

Activity C Answers may vary. Possible answer:

Yo me divierto en España. Es un lindo país. He hecho muchas cosas. He visitado la fuente mágica de Montjuic. Yo he comido en muchos buenos restaurantes. Yo he visto un concierto de jazz. Yo amo España.

¡Hasta pronto!
Samantha

Lesson 2

Activity A 1 a; 2 a; 3 b; 4 a

Activity B Answers may vary. Possible answers:

1 unos abrigos; 2 unos juguetes; 3 una camisa; 4 un perfume; 5 unos chocolates

Lesson 3

Activity A 1 Estamos en contacto.; 2 Yo me he divertido.; 3 Te voy a extrañar.; 4 ¡Hasta pronto!; 5 Ha sido un placer.

Activity B 1 próxima; 2 hospitalidad; 3 extrañar; 4 contacto; 5 divertido; 6 pronto
Bonus word: placer

Activity C 1 ¡Hasta la próxima!; 2 Ha sido un placer.; 3 Te voy a extrañar.

Lesson 4

Activity A Answers may vary. Possible answers:

1 Mi papá es más alto que mi mamá.; 2 El español es más difícil que el inglés.; 3 El pastel es mejor que la ensalada.; 4 El vino es mejor que la cerveza.; 5 Mi abuela es más linda que mi mamá.

Activity B 1 más; 2 tan; 3 menos

Activity C 1 más; 2 tan; 3 tan; 4 mejor

Lesson 5

Activity A 1 F; 2 F; 3 T; 4 T

Activity B Sí, yo estoy listo para salir.; Sí, me ha encantado la ciudad.; Sí, yo he visitado varios lugares.; ¡Adiós, nos vemos pronto!

Activity C 1 Sí, él ha hecho sus maletas.; 2 Sí, a él le ha gustado la ciudad.; 3 Sí, él ha visitado varios lugares.; 4 Sí, él ha comprado muchos regalos.

Lesson 6

Activity A Answers may vary. Possible answers:

1 El viaje fue genial.; 2 La comida estaba increíble.; 3 La ciudad era muy romántica.; 4 Los monumentos eran extraños.; 5 El espectáculo era divertido.

Activity B 1 interesante; 2 aburridas; 3 romántica; 4 horrible; 5 horroroso

Activity C buenos: divertido; delicioso; genial; magnífico
malos: horroroso; aburrido; horrible; espantoso
Your Turn
Answers will vary.

Lesson 7

Activity A 1 Yo me he quedado allí 6 días.; 2 Yo he ido a España.; 3 Estoy loco por ver las fotos.; 4 Estoy loco por regresar.

Activity B 1 a; 2 b; 3 a

Activity C Answers may vary. Possible answers:

1 Sí, yo he ido a España.; 2 Sí, yo he hecho muchos amigos.; 3 Sí, toda la gente ha sido amable.

Lesson 8

Activity A 1 Ellos se están quedando tres días en Mallorca.; 2 Ella está llegando a las tres de la mañana.; 3 Él se está divirtiendo.; 4 Yo estoy viniendo con mi familia.; 5 Nosotros estamos yendo al aeropuerto.

Activity B 1 está bajando; 2 están yendo; 3 está comiendo; 4 estamos haciendo; 5 estás subiendo

Activity C

venir	viniendo
salir	saliendo
quedar	quedando
llegar	llegando
leer	leyendo
pasar	pasando
bajar	bajando
caer	cayendo
nacer	naciendo

Review

Activity A Answers will vary. Possible answer:

Estoy en España. Me estoy divirtiendo. Los españoles son muy agradables. La comida es deliciosa. Estoy loco por volver.
¡Hasta pronto!
Brian

Activity B 1 más alto; 2 menos bella/más fea; 3 tan enfermo

Activity C 1 b; 2 b; 3 b; 4 b

Activity D Answers may vary. Possible answers:

1 Sí, yo me estoy divirtiendo.; 2 Yo estoy yendo a España.; 3 Me estoy quedando en el hotel.; 4 Me estoy quedando dos semanas.; 5 Estamos saliendo el 26 de octubre.
Challenge

Answers may vary. Possible answers:
estoy comprando; me estoy divirtiendo; estoy viniendo

Interior

p. 3: Zsolt Nyulaszi 2010/Shutterstock, Inc., pressmaster 2010/Fotolia, Rob Wilson 2008/Shutterstock, Inc., Noah Galen 2008/Shutterstock, Inc., microimages 2010/Fotolia, TessarTheTegu 2010/Fotolia; p. 4: Ivonne Wierink 2010/Fotolia, Andresr 2010/Shutterstock, Inc., Tomasz Trojanowski 2010/Shutterstock, Inc., Pres Panayotov 2010/Shutterstock, Inc., Losevsky Pavel 2008/Shutterstock, Inc.; p. 8: © Zsolt Nyulaszi 2010/Shutterstock, Inc.; p. 9: © herreneck 2010/Fotolia, vm 2008/Shutterstock, Inc., © BruceMash 2010/Fotolia, © Snowshill 2010/Fotolia, © Vibrant Image Studio 2008/Shutterstock, Inc., © Galyna Andrushko 2010/Fotolia, © Nabil BIYAHMADINE 2010/Fotolia, © Rob Wilson 2010/Shutterstock, Inc., © Blaz Kure 2008/Shutterstock, Inc., © TheSupe87 2010/Fotolia, © Mikael Damkier 2008/Shutterstock, Inc.; p. 10: © Rafael Ramirez Lee 2010/Shutterstock, Inc., © Nabil BIYAHMADINE 2010/Fotolia, © TheSupe87 2010/Fotolia, © Galyna Andrushko 2010/Fotolia, © vm 2008/Shutterstock, Inc.; p. 11: © Monkey Business Images 2010/Shutterstock, Inc., © Rob Wilson 2010/Shutterstock, Inc., © S.M. 2010/Shutterstock, Inc., © Lisa F. Young 2010/Shutterstock, Inc.; p.12: © Gemenacom 2010/Shutterstock, Inc., © Darryl Brooks 2008/Shutterstock, Inc., © Basov Mikhail 2010/Shutterstock, Inc., © kozvic49 2008/Shutterstock, Inc., © MANDY GODBEHEAR 2010/Shutterstock, Inc.; p.14: © Valeev 2010/Shutterstock, Inc., © Kristian Sekulic 2008/Shutterstock, Inc., © Gemenacom 2010/Shutterstock, Inc., © Ana Blazic 2008/Shutterstock, Inc., © Johnathan Larsen 2008/Shutterstock, Inc., © Luciano Mortula 2010/Shutterstock, Inc., © Manamana 2010/Shutterstock, Inc., © Ruta Saulyte 2010/Fotolia, © Daniel W. Slocum 2010/Shutterstock, Inc.; p. 16: © Mikael Damkier 2008/Shutterstock, Inc., © vm 2008/Shutterstock, Inc., © Rob Wilson 2010/Shutterstock, Inc., © Galyna Andrushko 2010/Fotolia; p. 17: © pressmaster 2010/Fotolia, © MaxFX 2008/Shutterstock, Inc.; p. 18: © Mike Flippo 2010/Fotolia, © Ewa Walicka 2010/Shutterstock, Inc., © Danny Smythe 2008/Fotolia, © AndersonRise 2010/Fotolia, © olly 2010/Fotolia; p. 19: © Yuri Arcurs 2010/Fotolia, © godfer 2010/Fotolia, © pressmaster 2010/Fotolia, © Wayne Johnson 2010/Fotolia, © Jamie Wilson 2010/Fotolia; p. 20: © Viorel Sima 2010/Shutterstock, Inc., © Yuri Arcurs 2008/Shutterstock, Inc.; p. 21: © DenisNata 2010/Shutterstock, Inc., © Andrey Brusov 2010/Fotolia; p. 22: © Robert Berry 2010/Shutterstock, Inc., © Yuri Arcurs 2008/Shutterstock, Inc., © Yuri Arcurs 2010/Shutterstock, Inc., © Vinicius Tupinamba 2010/Shutterstock, Inc.; p. 23: © Losevsky Pavel 2010/Shutterstock, Inc., © Kristian Sekulic 2008/Shutterstock, Inc., © Yuri Arcurs 2010/Fotolia, © Anton Gvozdikov 2010/Shutterstock, Inc., © moodboard3 2010/Fotolia, © Ersler Dmitry 2008/Shutterstock, Inc.; p. 24: © Fatini Zulnaidi 2008/Fotolia, © Snowshill 2010/Fotolia, © Diego Cervo 2008/Shutterstock, Inc., © Harris Shiffman 2010/Fotolia; p. 25: © Robert Berry 2010/Shutterstock, Inc., © Yuri Arcurs 2010/Shutterstock, Inc., © Vinicius Tupinamba 2010/Shutterstock, Inc.; p. 27: © Rob Wilson 2008/Shutterstock, Inc., © kozvic49 2008/Fotolia, TMAX 2010/Fotolia, © Claudia Petrilli/designbyclaudia.com; p. 28: © Gemenacom 2010/Shutterstock, Inc., © vm 2008/

Shutterstock, Inc., © Andresr 2008/Shutterstock, Inc., © Rob Wilson 2010/Shutterstock, Inc., © Darryl Brooks 2008/Shutterstock, Inc.; p. 29: © Monkey Business Images, © Maridav 2010/Fotolia, © AVAVA 2010/Fotolia, © Kruchankova Maya 2008/Shutterstock, Inc., © Edyta Pawlowska 2010/Fotolia; p. 30: © corepics 2010/Fotolia, © Lexx 2008/Shutterstock, Inc., © hfng 2010/Fotolia; p. 33: © Gemenacom 2010/Shutterstock, Inc., © Evgeny V. Kan 2008/Shutterstock, Inc., © vm 2008/Shutterstock, Inc., © Norman Pogson 2010/Fotolia, © Danny Smythe 2008/Fotolia, © Lexx 2008/Shutterstock, Inc., © Hannu Lilvaar 2008/Shutterstock, Inc., © Yuri Arcurs 2008/Shutterstock, Inc.; p. 34: © Danny Smythe 2008/Fotolia, © Snowshill 2010/Fotolia, © Hannu Lilvaar 2008/Shutterstock, Inc.; p. 35: © Noah Galen 2008/Shutterstock, Inc.; p. 36: © robert lerich 2010/Fotolia, © Gordana Sermek 2010/Shutterstock, Inc., © Vladislav Gajic 2010/Fotolia, © Margo Harrison 2010/Shutterstock, Inc., © Kwest 2010/Fotolia; p. 37: © TessarTheTegu 2010/Fotolia; p. 38: © Phase4Photography 2008/Shutterstock, Inc., © Yuri Arcurs 2008/Shutterstock, Inc., © Michael Shake 2010/Fotolia, © Vitaliy Pakhnyushchyy 2010/Fotolia, © Vinicius Tupinamba 2010/Fotolia, © Lai Leng Yiap 2010/Fotolia, © idrutu 2010/Fotolia, © Peter Albrektsen 2010/Fotolia; p. 40: © Larry Lawhead 2010/Fotolia, © Ambrose 2010/Fotolia, OlgaLIS 2010/Fotolia, © Valeriy Velikov 2010/Fotolia, © Alexey Khromushin 2010/Fotolia, © auremar 2010/Fotolia, © Mazzzur 2010/Fotolia, © Valeriy Velikov 2010/Fotolia; p. 41: © Gemenacom 2010/Shutterstock, Inc., © Photoobjects 2008/Shutterstock, Inc., © iofoto 2010/Shutterstock, Inc., © Dusan Zidar 2008/Shutterstock, Inc., © Diana Lundin 2010/Shutterstock, Inc.; p. 42: © Arrow Studio, © Phase4Photography 2008/Shutterstock, Inc., © EuToch 2010/Fotolia, © Larry Lawhead 2010/Fotolia, © idrutu 2010/Fotolia; p. 44: microimages 2010/Fotolia; p. 45: © Miguel Raurich/Iberimage.com, © Viktoria 2010/Shutterstock, Inc., © Jimmy818 2010/Fotolia, © 3d brained 2010/Fotolia, © designer_things 2010/Fotolia; p. 46: © Artur Marciniec 2010/Fotolia; p. 47: © Andrzej Tokarski 2010/Fotolia; p. 48: © 26kot 2010/Shutterstock, Inc.; p. 49: © 2008 Shutterstock, Inc., © mtrommer 2010/Fotolia, © mtrommer 2010/Fotolia, © Tatiana 2010/Fotolia, © detmering design 2010/Fotolia; p. 50: © Diego Cervo 2008/Shutterstock, Inc., © Justin Paget 2010/Fotolia; p. 51: © Edyta Pawlowska 2008/Shutterstock, Inc., © Andriy Goncharenko 2008/Shutterstock, Inc., © 2008 Shutterstock, Inc., © sean cashman 2010/Fotolia; p. 52: © Andrei Nekrassov 2010/Fotolia, © redslice 2010/Fotolia, © Viktoria 2010/Shutterstock, Inc., © designer_things 2010/Fotolia; p. 53: © TessarTheTegu 2010/Fotolia; p. 54: © Keith Wheatley 2008/Shutterstock, Inc., © klikk 2010/Fotolia, © Paul Maguire 2008/Shutterstock, Inc., © Ewa Brozek 2010/Fotolia, © Alexander Bryljaev 2010/Fotolia, © Joe Gough 2008/Shutterstock, Inc., © Joe Gough 2008/Shutterstock, Inc.; p. 55: © Comstock, © Keith Wheatley 2008/Shutterstock, Inc.; p. 56: © Liv Friis-Larsen 2008/Shutterstock, Inc., © Stepanov 2008/Shutterstock, Inc., © Comstock; p. 57: © Sergey Rusakov 2008/Shutterstock, Inc., © Frelon 2010/Fotolia, © Joe Gough 2008/Shutterstock, Inc., © Joe Gough 2008/Shutterstock, Inc., © Viktor1 2008/Shutterstock, Inc., © Luminis 2010/Fotolia, ©